THE
UNSOLVED
CASE FILES OF
SHERLOCK
HOLMES

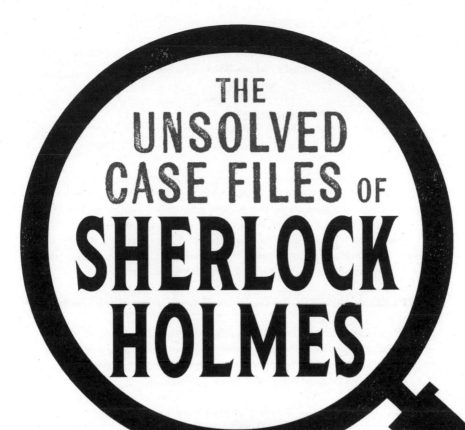

THE UNSOLVED CASE FILES OF SHERLOCK HOLMES

25 CRYPTIC PUZZLES

STEWART ROSS

Michael O'Mara Books Limited

This edition first published in paperback in 2023
First published as *Solve it Like Sherlock* in Great Britain in 2018 by
Michael O'Mara Books Limited
9 Lion Yard
Tremadoc Road
London SW4 7NQ

A CIP catalogue record for this book is available from the British Library.

Papers used by Michael O'Mara Books Limited are natural,
recyclable products made from wood grown in sustainable forests.
The manufacturing processes conform to the environmental
regulations of the country of origin.

ISBN 978-1-78929-587-0 in paperback print format
ISBN 978-1-78243-943-1 in ebook format

1 3 5 7 9 10 8 6 4 2

Cover picture credits: Shutterstock
Cover designed by Natasha Le Coultre
Typeset by Ed Pickford
Illustration on pages 19, 43, 68, 86, 101, 113, 117, 120,
121, 133, 150, 177, 191 by Paul Collicutt

Printed and bound by CPI Group (UK) Ltd, Croydon, CR0 4YY

Follow us on Twitter @OMaraBooks

www.mombooks.com

To my brother Charlie Ross, the TV auctioneer,
with grateful thanks for his help with the Missing
Masterpieces.

CONTENTS

INTRODUCTION

The number of cases Sherlock Holmes tackled is unknown. Between them, Dr Watson and the famous detective wrote up fifty-six as short stories and a further four as full-length novels. However, in 'The Adventure of the Solitary Cyclist', the doctor mentions taking 'very full notes' on 'hundreds of private cases' undertaken by Holmes between 1894 and 1901.

Imagine my surprise and delight, therefore, when an unknown benefactor left on my doorstep a large bundle of Watson's original work relating to many of the cases that had never made it into the novels or collections of stories.

What was I to do with them? At first, I considered expanding them into a new casebook, reproducing as closely as possible the style of the original. The idea did not last long. I feel a strong antipathy towards pastiche, and believe that adding to the Collected Works would be akin to desecration.

The notes could have been published unedited, in the disorderly form in which I found them, but the result would have been of interest only to scholars and obsessive

Holmesians. The solution I eventually hit upon arose as I considered how Sherlock Holmes's timeless appeal rested largely on the enjoyment readers took from his extraordinary crime-solving powers.

Holmes's success rested on (i) his remarkable powers of deduction, founded solely on reason, and (ii) a formidable bank of information stored within his computer-like brain. (Interestingly, as I read through the notes, I found myself concurring with Watson's observation in *A Study in Scarlet*: Holmes's knowledge, like that of an encyclopaedia with some of its pages missing, had surprising gaps.)

This proviso notwithstanding, my presentation of the twenty-five new cases in this book focuses on Holmes's world-famous ability to solve crimes through logical reasoning and knowledge. Each story is set out in two parts. The narrative at the front of the book contains the information Holmes required to do his job. Watson's notes, though full, do not display the range of colourful detail – descriptions of Holmes's room in Baker Street, for example – that he used to turn *cases* into *detective stories*. In general, therefore, I have resisted the temptation to embellish objective fact with imaginative fiction. Words taken verbatim from Watson's notes are set out as quotes. Elsewhere we have used standard contemporary English, moderating it where appropriate to suit the epoch and subject matter.

I invite you, using the techniques Holmes made famous, to uncover for yourself the evidence in each story and use it to unravel the mystery. When you believe you have done so, turn to the back of the book. There you will find out how Holmes correctly interpreted the facts to solve twenty-four of the twenty-five cases.

Perhaps you can go one better? Good luck!

Stewart Ross

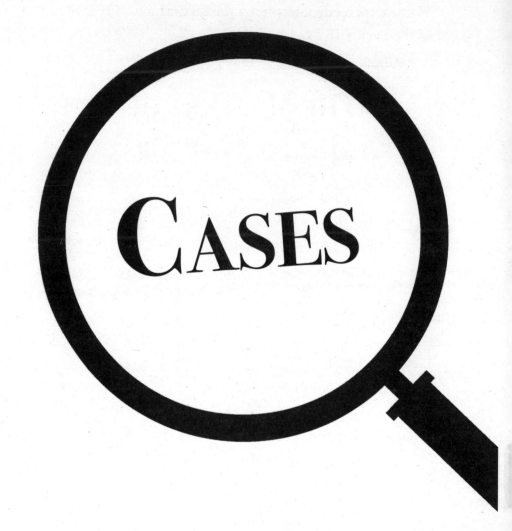

THE MYSTERY OF
BARON GALTÜR

As Sherlock Holmes's fame spread around the world, he received a steady stream of correspondence from more than a dozen nations. Most came from individuals seeking his help in solving some arcane mystery. The genesis of the story that Watson provisionally entitled 'The Adventure of Baron Galtür' was different. It lay not in the failure of the Austrian police to solve a crime, but in Baron Galtür's insistence that they had arrested the wrong man.

Holmes's attention to the case was drawn by a letter, postmarked Interlaken, that reached Baker Street on 25 February 1887. 'Interesting,' Holmes said to Watson as he picked up the envelope and examined it. 'You will note from the crinkling of the paper that this envelope has been steamed open after posting.' Either it contained matters of political significance, he went on, or it was written by someone in prison.

He was correct, of course. The letter was written by an Austrian nobleman, Frederich Hoffbilt, Baron Galtür, who had been detained in His Imperial Majesty's prison, Interlaken, pending trial for murder. The notes that Watson took from his letter to Holmes, which the doctor said was written in formal, rather old-fashioned and stilted English, are easily summarized.

The baron had been arrested for killing a young aristocrat, Egmont von Wasptakker. He admitted that the evidence against him, although circumstantial, was overwhelming; and yet he insisted to 'the most esteemed and honourable of detectives' that he was, 'in the name of Almighty God Himself and of His Holy Mother Maria, innocent of this terrible crime'.

The letter concluded by beseeching the Englishman – the baron's 'only hoping' – to contact the Viennese lawyer who was acting on his behalf: the man, 'a respectable servant of justice', had been instructed to pass on to Holmes full details of a case that was 'the breaking of my heart as was already done to that of my beloved daughter, Elizabeth'.

Holmes considered the letter carefully for a while and came to two conclusions. First, the baron was almost certainly not guilty of the murder of which he stood accused: if he were indeed guilty, he would not be calling upon the services of a detective renowned for his unfailing ability to uncover the truth. Second, as Holmes could not spare the time to travel to Austria, he relished the unusual challenge of tackling a case by correspondence. Watson said it could not be done, Holmes bet him five guineas that it could, and the pair shook hands on the wager.

On receipt of a request from Holmes, the baron's Viennese lawyer replied with an excellent, fifteen-page account of the murder and its attendant circumstances. In a short paragraph at the beginning, he said he would try to be wholly objective so that the London detective could see for himself how desperately incontrovertible the evidence against his client appeared to be.

The baron's family had lived in the remote Austrian village of Galtür since the time of the Emperor Charles V. They owned large estates there and had the reputation of being fair if somewhat paternalistic landlords. The baron's wife had died eighteen years ago, shortly after the birth of their only child, Elizabeth. Frederich Hoffbilt had not remarried but channelled his affection on to his daughter who, under his watchful but loving eye, had grown up into a very beautiful young lady.

In the summer of the previous year, 1886, a pair of young brothers from Vienna had rented one of the baron's hunting lodges as a base from which to go walking in the mountains. Though the names would mean nothing to Holmes, the lawyer explained, they carried great weight in Austria. George and Egmont von Wasptakker, distant cousins of the ruling Habsburg dynasty, were wealthy, privileged and used to getting their own way. In terms of status and influence, they towered over a provincial nobleman. The lawyer confessed that the disparity of influence made his task all the harder.

On reading this, Watson noted, Holmes muttered something about Magna Carta and all men being equal under the law.

By the end of their stay in Galtür, George and Egmont were clearly smitten by the charms of Elizabeth Hoffbilt, and spent a good deal more time hanging around the baron's castle than walking on the hills. During the autumn, much to her father's annoyance, Elizabeth received several letters from both young men. They reappeared in the district shortly before Christmas and, when the baron said his hunting lodges were no longer available, took rooms at an inn just four hundred yards from his castle. They had come, they said,

to engage in the increasingly fashionable sport of skiing. As the lawyer wryly noted, the sport they were actually engaged in was a good deal older.

At this point the account offered a brief character sketch of each of the two young suitors. The twenty-one-year-old George was serious-minded, scholarly, moral and deeply religious. The lawyer waxed unusually poetic in his description, saying the passionate young man had 'pursued the fair Elizabeth like a medieval knight, sworn to fight the fiercest dragon to win the hand of the fair maiden upon whom his heart was set'. He attended mass regularly and was considering a career as a university professor. Though handsome in a dark, chiselled manner, he gave the impression of being over-earnest and somewhat humourless.

Egmont, two years younger than his brother, could hardly have been more different. He was charming, with bright blue eyes, fair hair and a quick, mobile face. The lawyer intimated that, back in Vienna, Egmont consorted with a group of wealthy young army officers whose only interests were in drinking and chasing girls. Moreover, it was rumoured that he had privately sworn to marry three young ladies, but had not honoured his promise to wed one of them. From the moment they first met, Baron Galtur had made his dislike of the young profligate quite clear. Unfortunately, this had only served to make Egmont even keener in his pursuit of Elizabeth.

Matters came to a head in early February when the family doctor broke his oath of confidentiality and informed the baron that his daughter was 'with child'. When questioned, Elizabeth confessed that Egmont, whom she loved dearly and wished to marry, was responsible for her condition: the couple had been meeting in secret almost every night since his return to Galtür. So he could get into the castle undetected, she had given him a key to the servants' entrance.

On hearing his daughter's confession, fury mingled with despair in the nobleman's breast. The weather was unusually mild for the time of year and, without pausing even to pull on a coat, he hurried through the melting snow to the isolated inn where the two brothers were staying. The confrontation between the father and the lover can easily be imagined: the older man demanded that Egmont marry his daughter immediately; the latter played it cool, saying there was no proof that he was responsible for Elizabeth's pregnancy – could it not have been his brother, George, who was even keener on the girl than he was? – and adding that any marriage would require the approval of his parents, who would almost certainly not accept 'a provincial nobody, no matter how beautiful' into their family.

At this the baron lost all self-control. He yelled at Egmont, calling him a vile and heartless puppy and swearing to kill him. The threat was shouted loudly enough to be clearly heard by George, whose suite was next door, and by Jan Flugger, the innkeeper. When questioned by the police the following day, both men gave precisely the same account of what had happened.

It was already getting dark when the baron stormed out of the inn. The temperature had dropped markedly, transforming the water trickling from the eaves into pointed, glassy stalactites, and turning the snow to a crystal carpet that crunched beneath his feet. Shortly after he reached his castle, it snowed heavily until around midnight. A severe frost then set in, and the temperature remained below freezing for the next five days.

It was Egmont's custom to have his breakfast served in his room no earlier than eleven o'clock each morning. When, at about 11.15, Jan Flugger collected a tray of bread and fruit and knocked at Egmont's door, there was no reply. As this was not uncommon, he put down the tray, pushed open the unlocked door and peered inside. He was immediately struck by how cold the room was. The window was wide open and, as might be expected, the fire had burned itself out many hours before and even the ashes were cold. Flugger coughed politely and advanced towards the bed. His guest appeared to be still asleep, lying on his back with his arms flung wide across the bedclothes. It was not until the innkeeper drew back the curtains that he noticed the blood – Egmont von Wasptakker was dead, killed by a single thrust of a sharp spike that had pierced his carotid artery.

Galtür had only one policeman, an elderly and corpulent officer who had never been confronted by a murder. However, he did have the wit to order no one to approach the inn or the baron's castle, for in the fresh snow he had noticed footprints indicative of four journeys between the two venues – evidence that might be of interest to the detectives summoned from Interlaken. The impressions certainly did interest them, as did something else they noticed in the Great Hall of Baron Galtür's castle.

There were two very clear sets of footprints. One, confirmed by matching the boots of the deceased to the frozen indentations, had been made by Egmont. They showed him walking, sometime after midnight, from the inn to the servants' entrance of the castle and back again. The second set of prints was made by the baron walking from the front door of his castle to the inn and then returning home, for the marks accurately matched a pair of his footwear.

From this evidence, the Interlaken detectives deduced that Egmont had gone to visit Elizabeth after the snowstorm had stopped and then returned home. The baron, seething with anger at the young man's insolent continuation of his relationship with his daughter, had followed him back to the inn, killed him, and retreated to his castle. And the murder weapon? Careful examination of the weaponry displayed on the walls of the baron's great hall revealed that one of the bayonets had recently been wiped clean. All the others were covered in dust.

The only piece of evidence in the baron's favour, concluded the lawyer, was that the wretched Elizabeth, now beside herself with grief, had sworn that Egmont had not visited her that night. The detectives dismissed this, saying that either she was lying or the baron had been waiting for Egmont by the servants' door and had driven him off before he could meet up with his lover.

'Strange as it may seem, my dear Watson,' said Holmes after he had read the letter three times, 'I believe the poor girl was telling the truth.'

After giving the matter further thought, he wrote a long reply to the baron's lawyer suggesting what had really happened on the night of the murder. Four weeks later he received a letter from the baron himself. It thanked him 'from the deepest region of my heart' for furnishing his lawyer with the line of enquiry that had led to his client's release and the discovery of the true villain.

What could Holmes have said in his letter to the Viennese lawyer?

THE ADVENTURE OF THE
ADELAIDE STAR

One of the most distinctive cases we came across while trawling through Watson's notes begins with the sad demise of a well-known Australian entrepreneur. Travelling to Britain on the *Adelaide Star*, Mr Edward Thriepland died of a heart attack four days after the vessel had left Cape Town. In accordance with the wishes of Mrs Thriepland, who was travelling with her fifty-three-year-old husband, his body was buried at sea.

That, in the normal run of things, would have been that. But it wasn't.

An hour after the last passenger had disembarked at Southampton, a middle-aged Australian woman came aboard the *Adelaide Star* and asked to speak to the captain. Where was her husband? she demanded.

Her husband? echoed the confused Penprase. When his visitor responded by bursting into tears of pain and fury, it gradually dawned on him that he was addressing the real Mrs Thriepland. The much younger woman who had accompanied her husband on the voyage from Australia was an imposter. She had since disappeared and left no contact details.

The aggrieved widow contacted the police. They were sympathetic but said that, although adultery might be morally criminal, it was not against the law. Nor had the false Mrs Thriepland gone off with Mr Thriepland's luggage, all of which had been delivered to his London address. However, they would keep an eye open for the imposter as she had very probably travelled on a forged passport.

Upon reflection, Mrs Thriepland was not greatly surprised by her late husband's behaviour. Since moving to England with her, fifteen years earlier, he had frequently been away from home on business, and had twice gone back and forth to Australia on his own. She was sure he had spent time with other women, too, but as long as he funded her lavish London lifestyle and did not create a scandal, she didn't much care what he did.

Five months later, Mrs Thriepland received a letter. Postmarked Melbourne, it had been sent by Mr Aldous Grang, the manager of Colonial Gems, one of the Thriepland enterprises in Australia. After offering the customary condolences, Grang asked about the diamonds Mr Thriepland had been bringing back to England with him. Grang assumed the jewels, worth an estimated £100,000, had been handed over to Mrs Thriepland with the rest of her husband's effects, but as Grang had not heard anything, would she mind confirming their safe arrival in writing?

On reading Grang's letter, Mrs Thriepland went straight to Sherlock Holmes. Watson tells us she was 'large', 'formidable', and 'very, very angry' with the woman she described as a 'scheming dingo' who had seduced her husband and impersonated her, his wife, in order to steal the diamonds.

Holmes listened to the tirade but made no comment. Did Mrs Thriepland have any of her late husband's effects that might help his enquiry? he asked. In response, she showed him a telegram Mr Thriepland had sent to 'the thieving hussy' on the day the couple set sail from Melbourne. Found by a cleaner beneath the bed in the couple's stateroom and subsequently forwarded to the real Mrs Thriepland by the shipping line, it showed, she said, the extent to which the imposter had got her husband under her thumb. She had even sweet-talked him into using a 'soppy, lovey-dovey nickname'. Hitherto, Mr Thriepland had insisted on being 'Edward', never 'Teddy'.

The telegram ran:

MY NAUGHTY LITTLE DARLING STOP WHAT AN ADVENTURE STOP AM WITH YOU ON BOARD AND EVER AFTER STOP SPEAK TO ME WITH YOUR BRILLIANT EYES STOP OUR FUTURE GLEAMS STOP BE THE LOVING WIFE AND LEAVE ALL THE REST TO ME STOP YOUR DEVOTED TEDDY

Holmes read the telegram carefully. After taking notes on the case and arranging for Mrs Thriepland to pay a handsome fee if he were successful, he said he would do his best to recover her property. He warned that it might take some time.

Watson recorded Holmes's investigation under five headings. The first was simply HATTON GARDEN. It indicated that Holmes had begun by asking a friend who worked in London's jewellery quarter whether there had been any suspicious dealings in diamonds over the previous few months. From the response he learned 'some chap with a colonial accent' had been making enquiries about selling unmounted diamonds.

The second heading was ORIENTAL AND COLONIAL, the name of the company operating the *Adelaide Star*. From their offices in Great Portland Street, Holmes came away with two names he believed would be useful to him: Captain Jago Penprase and Dr Hogwin E. Palfrey. The master of the *Adelaide Star*, who had been with the line for thirty years, was currently on leave in his native Cornwall. Palfrey was the doctor who had attended Mr Thriepland during his final hours. He was not a regular with O & C, but had joined the ship as a replacement when its full-time doctor had suddenly been taken ill and had to stay behind in Melbourne.

CAPTAIN PENPRASE was the third heading. Holmes travelled down to Cornwall by train and met with the old salt in his home overlooking Newlyn harbour. The captain was still irritated that O & C had accepted a passenger travelling under a forged passport, and offered to help the inquiry in any way he could.

Yes, he remembered the telegram arriving for the passenger travelling as 'Mrs Thriepland'. He remembered, too, that on the evening Mr Thriepland was taken ill, he and his supposed wife were due to dine with him at the captain's table. She had sent a message around 7 p.m. saying that, regretfully, as her husband was unwell, neither of them would be at dinner that evening. She sent for the ship's doctor around 10 p.m., and her husband had died a few minutes past midnight. The captain had been informed immediately. On entering the couple's stateroom, he found Mrs Thriepland

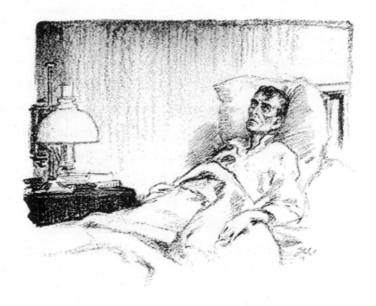

weeping quietly in a chair. The stewardess had brought her a drink and was doing her best to comfort her.

Dr Palfrey was also present. He told the captain he had attended Mr Thriepland at 10.05 p.m. and found him suffering from a severe stomach disorder. He had given him an injection of morphine to ease the pain, and had returned to his quarters. Going to check on his patient shortly before midnight, he found him pale and vomiting. He recognized the symptoms of a severe heart attack but was unable to help. Mr Thriepland died shortly afterwards.

The regulations stipulated that the master of the ship confirm the doctor's pronouncement. When Penprase checked for a pulse on the 'deathly pale' body, he found the wrist 'cold, lifeless and dry'. There were traces of vomit around the mouth.

The captain recalled how Mrs Thriepland was most insistent that her husband's body be buried at sea. It was, she said, 'just what he would have wanted'. Moreover, she believed a swift ceremony would help her come to terms with her loss. Sobbing bitterly, she said she could not bear the thought of sailing on a vessel with her husband's dead body 'rotting somewhere down below'.

In conversation with the captain a few days after the committal, Dr Palfrey confessed to having been badly shaken by the incident. The responsibility of being the sole medical man on board was very burdensome, and he had decided to leave O & C when they arrived in England and set up as a family doctor. Penprase was not surprised. He had found Palfrey a 'cold fish', not at all suited to the convivial life on board an ocean liner.

Watson offers one further piece of information from the Penprase interview. When the ship docked at Southampton, the false Mrs Thriepland had refused all assistance and gone ashore on her own, carrying only a small valise. She left no forwarding address.

NANCY DENNE, the fourth of Watson's headings, was the stewardess allocated to the Thriepland stateroom. She too had been upset by the death of Mr Thriepland, though she confessed to having found the man 'a bit of a brute'. At the end of the voyage, she had left O & C to marry her long-standing fiancé, Herbert Denne, with whom she now ran a small tobacconist's in Portsmouth.

Nancy Denne's version of events was similar in almost all respects to that of Captain Penprase. She had found the attractive, red-headed woman travelling as Mrs Thriepland 'pleasant, but a little nervous'. The doctor she described as 'quiet and professional', adding that he was 'quite a looker'. When she had gone into the stateroom around 10 p.m. to see how Mr Thriepland was doing, he was lying in bed with his so-called wife sitting at his right side, holding his hand. The sick man had groaned and waved his free arm in her direction. 'Like he was calling me towards him,' Nancy recalled.

His mistress – 'that's what we know she was, don't we?' – said her husband was delirious and asked Nancy to fetch Dr Palfrey. She found him eating almond macaroons (she clearly remembered the smell) and begged him to attend Mr Thriepland without delay. He snatched up his bag, which was standing packed and ready on a table by the door, and followed her to the stairway leading to the first-class accommodation.

Watson's fifth heading was DOCTOR PALFREY. Having tracked him down through the General Medical Council register, Holmes arrived at the small Yorkshire town where he practised to find the place in mourning. The doctor's wife, a young, red-headed woman who had been ill for the past month, had passed away two days previously. The funeral was arranged for the following day.

Holmes went promptly to the nearest police station.

Taking an officer with him, he then called in at the funeral parlour of Herbert Braithwaite & Sons, the local undertaker. That afternoon, searches were made and culminated in an arrest.

Ten days later, the police handed over the missing diamonds to Mrs Thriepland, and she handed over a large cheque to Sherlock Holmes.

How had he earned it?

THE MYSTERY OF THE STABBED SHAKESPEAREAN

Watson's notes contain some very catchy titles. They are so good, in fact, that occasionally we found the stories that followed – in note form – something of a disappointment. Such tales rarely made it into the published works.

This was not the case with 'The Mystery of the Stabbed Shakespearean'. The doctor probably did not use it as a full-length story because he had insufficient detail on the setting and characters. We are more concerned with deduction than personality and fine phrases. Consequently, from Watson's scanty jottings we have been able to construct what we believe is a neat little puzzle. It is also one that shows, as we point out in 'A Case of Ignorance', Holmes to have been better read than Watson suggested in *A Study in Scarlet*.

The problem is simply stated.

Professor Algernon Thomas, widely acknowledged as the finest Shakespearean scholar of his generation, was cruelly murdered in his rooms at Gloucester College, Oxford. He died of a single, skilful stab by a sharp instrument that pierced his left eye and entered his brain.

The body was discovered at 10.30 a.m. by a student who had come for a tutorial on the Bard's adaptation of Holinshed. The young man found the door leading off the stone staircase slightly ajar and, assuming that deafness – not death – explained the lack of response to his knocks, he pushed open the door and peered inside. The professor's body lay on its back with its arms by its side. A doctor said it had lain there for at least twelve hours.

Three red smears suggested that, after withdrawing the murder weapon from the eye socket, the assassin had attempted to wipe it clean on the dead man's shirt front. Items of interest in the room included an empty port bottle, a half-empty bottle of the same beverage, two crystal drinking glasses dirtied only by a few dregs at the bottom of each, and an open and torn copy of Shakespeare's *Henry VI, Part 2.*

We are not told how Holmes became involved in the case, but we assume that an inexperienced detective from the Oxfordshire force, overwhelmed by the condescending atmosphere of Gloucester College and its irascible fellows, had begged the famous London detective for assistance. Holmes was ever willing to join the fray against pretension and privilege, and agreed to help. He arrived in Oxford at 10.53 a.m. and departed at 6.47 p.m., having solved the murder.

Holmes had swiftly narrowed the list of suspects down to two. The first, and the one the Master of the College wished to see 'dragged to the stake on a hurdle', was Hélène La Chaise, a fiery, twenty-one-year-old French woman whose bourgeois parents, disapproving of her affair with a prominent Parisian politician, had packed her off to Oxford eighteen months previously 'to improve her English'. She was soon seen tripping elegantly – and only partially disguised as a male student – up the stone staircase that led to Professor Thomas's rooms. Six months after her arrival, the rouge-lipped, elegantly attired *Française* was widely but never publicly acknowledged to be his mistress.

The relationship was stormy, especially when Hélène demanded money from her much older lover as proof of his affection. The situation was further complicated when, on one of her frequent trips to London, she became secretly engaged to John Ruthwell, the second son of the fabulously wealthy Bishop of Durham. Though she managed to keep her lucrative Oxford dalliance from her straight-laced fiancé, the professor's ecclesiastical colleagues warned him, albeit tactfully and obliquely, that he was being cuckolded.

The porter had seen Hélène, wearing her usual half-hearted disguise, going up to the professor's rooms at about 6.30 p.m. on the evening of the murder. No one had seen her leave. She said she had argued with Thomas, whom she had found 'more of a mean *paysan* than a *professeur*', and returned to her apartment near the Parks to prepare for a trip to London the following day. The police found a pair of sharp steel knitting needles in a chest of drawers in her bedroom. She had no interest in knitting, she said, and believed the needles had been left in the apartment by its previous occupant.

Although the murder took place in July, when most of the college rooms were deserted, a postgraduate student, returning at about 10.30 p.m. from a convivial evening with friends in Hertford College, remembered hearing Professor Thomas's angry voice emanating from his open window. He had taken little notice at the time, but later recalled hearing 'Helen' quite distinctly. He also heard 'debt', either as a single word or as part of a longer one, and 'butter'. On being questioned further, he admitted that 'butter' might have been 'but a'.

Watson notes that though these scattered syllables were 'not much to go on', they furnished his friend with 'important though ambiguous clues'.

The second of Holmes's suspects was a visiting American academic from Yale. Like Professor Thomas, Professor Tippington Wynberg III was a Shakespearean; but unlike his English counterpart, he was convinced that Christopher Marlowe, not the man from Stratford, was the true author of the finest plays in the English language.

His appearance at the college was preceded by the delivery of three large packing cases stuffed with all kinds of scholarly – and not so scholarly – paraphernalia. This included two busts of Marlowe, several manuscripts, 105 leather-bound books, a golden quill pen that Wynberg carried in his pocket to write neo-Elizabethan sonnets 'when the muse was upon him', a full-length portrait of his late wife, and a print of Canterbury Cathedral viewed from the King's School, Marlowe's alma mater.

Wynberg's public lecture on Marlowe's authorship of Shakespeare, delivered before an august audience on 13 May, was coolly received. The American already had a reputation as a heavy drinker, and he was rumoured to have been at the bottle long before he took to the podium. Professor Thomas, the lecture's most vitriolic critic, said he would shortly publish a paper 'demonstrating beyond all doubt that Wynberg was a fool and a fraud'.

From that moment onwards, the two men did not exchange a civil word. On four separate occasions, the American stood in the quadrangle below the Englishman's rooms and challenged him to 'come out and fight'. Each time, Thomas opened his window and poured foul water and even fouler abuse on his enemy's head.

On the night of the murder, Wynberg said he had stayed in his rooms until about 11.00 p.m., when he had gone out into the quadrangle for a breath of fresh air. He was not seen near the stairway leading to Professor Thomas's rooms, but the porter recalled bumping into him in the quadrangle around 11.15 p.m. The American had been 'acting very strangely', he said. With his hands clasped tightly behind his back, and staring intently down at his feet, Wynberg walked round and round the quadrangle muttering repeatedly, 'I spy my foot, I spy my foot.'

The Oxford detective suggested to Holmes that the evidence strongly pointed to Hélène La Chaise as the killer. She had done the deed, he said, when Thomas refused further money (presumably saying he would no longer service her 'debt') and threatened to denounce her to her puritanical fiancé. The professor had even been overheard shouting her name shortly before his demise.

Holmes agreed that this was the obvious reading of the case, but believed it was only one possible interpretation. In his view, the murderer could just as easily have been Norman Wynberg III. He based his remark on an alternative reading of the words gleaned from the postgraduate student and college porter. Holmes admitted his version was not conclusive, but its veracity would be confirmed if a microscopic examination of an object from the American's rooms provided the evidence he was anticipating.

Unsurprisingly, Holmes's construing of the puzzling words and phrases was proved correct. After a close analysis of one of Wynberg's possessions, he was arrested and charged with murder.

How had Holmes interpreted the words overheard by the postgraduate student and the college porter, and what object of Wynberg's did he ask to be microscopically examined?

THE LADY FROM KENT

Monday 12 January 1891 was a cold, blustery day in which sharp showers alternated with short moments of winter sunshine. In the late afternoon, during one of these brighter interludes, Watson called at 221B Baker Street to find his friend Sherlock Holmes in an unusually unsettled mood. He was pacing impatiently about the room, pausing every now and again to glance out of the window into the street below. He was doing precisely this as Watson came in, and the doctor noted how the red-orange glow of the setting sun gave his friend's sharp features an almost devilish appearance.

It seems that Holmes was waiting for one of his Baker Street Irregulars to arrive with information relating to a case he was working on at the time. To Holmes's annoyance, the boy never appeared. Watson never tells us why, because his attention was diverted by the arrival at 221B of a most striking new client.

'Ah, Watson! We have a caller,' announced the detective during one of his forays to the window. 'I see a cab has come to a halt just below my window and a lady has alighted on to the pavement. She is currently checking the numbers on the houses, and I expect Mrs Hudson will shortly be announcing her.'

Two minutes later an attractive, fair-haired young woman of around twenty-five was shown into the room and, upon Holmes's invitation, took a seat opposite him. She appeared agitated, and, as soon as she was seated, she begged my friend's assistance to prevent a murder. At this, the detective sat back in his chair, fixed her with his eagle stare, and bade her explain further. Her dramatic declaration had clearly aroused his interest.

The lady, who introduced herself as Mrs Elizabeth Flowers of Tunbridge Wells, Kent, wore an elegant, close-fitting dark grey dress drawn in tight at the waist, with a high collar and frills of lace at the cuffs. Her expensive boots had been splashed by dirt from the street and there was a small faded patch on the upper toe of the left boot, as if it had been scorched when left to dry by the fire. Apart from her wedding ring, her only adornment was a string of handsome pearls. Watson also noted that, although she was distinctly good-looking, Mrs Flowers' attractiveness was somewhat lessened by the abnormally dark circles beneath her eyes. These were explained when she confessed that, overcome by anxiety, she had 'hardly slept a wink' during the past fortnight.

The lady's husband, Edward Flowers, was a lawyer who divided his time between his practice in the country and consultancy work in London. The couple had been married for five years and had no children. Though Edward still worked, she explained that he had no need to do so as he had recently come into a considerable sum of money. Therein lay the source of her anxiety.

Early the previous year, Edward's father, Lambert Flowers, a wealthy widower who had made his fortune in South Africa, had been found dead in his country house near the small Kentish town of Tenterden. There were no marks upon the body and foul play was not suspected. He was a large man with a penchant for fine Scotch whisky, a half-drunk glass of which remained on the table near where he fell. His drinking, coupled with lack of exercise, led the local doctor to conclude he had died of a heart attack. At the time, Mrs Flowers said, she had no reason to question the diagnosis.

This seemed to upset her, and she broke down in a fit of most pitiable sobbing. After a sip of brandy from Holmes's decanter, she slowly recovered, carefully dried her eyes, and continued with her story.

The whole of Lambert Flowers' considerable fortune passed to his elder son, Wincott, Mrs Flowers' bachelor brother-in-law. She said that neither she nor her husband resented Wincott's inheritance, as Edward's earnings brought in ample for them to enjoy a very comfortable life.

At this point, Watson wrote down her precise words: 'Though we felt no jealousy for Wincott's good fortune, Lambert's brother, Gregory, was a great deal less charitable. I heard him say quite plainly that at least half the money should have come to him as payment for taking care of Lambert's house and affairs while he was away in South Africa.'

Mrs Flowers went on to tell Holmes and Watson a little more about Gregory Flowers. A resident of the nearby village of Goudhurst, he was a chemist and inventor who made a reasonable living by selling his patented discoveries to companies employed in the armaments and medical industries. He had married young but his wife had left him just a fortnight after the wedding for reasons that were never explained. Mrs Elizabeth Flowers, who had for a short time before her marriage worked as an assistant in Gregory

Flowers' laboratory, believed she knew why he now lived alone. He had a habit, she explained with a shudder, of treating his female staff with 'rather more than common courtesy'.

Holmes nodded and requested she continue.

On 27 September, barely half a year after Lambert Flowers' sudden death, his elder son Wincott was struck down in a similar fashion – found dead at his dinner table with a half-finished glass of red wine beside him. Again, no marks on the body and no obvious suspicion of foul play. An autopsy report stated that he had been in sound health. However, suspicious compounds discovered in his stomach along with the partly digested remains of his dinner suggested he may have been poisoned.

The police questioned Gregory Flowers, who pleaded innocent and provided a sound alibi for the time in question. With no firm evidence to go on, the police closed the investigation, and Wincott Flowers was declared to have died, 'probably by poison administered by person or persons unknown'.

Here, Mrs Flowers broke down again. For a second time, she was revived by Holmes's brandy before she delicately dabbed her eyes and continued.

Wincott's will left the family fortune to his brother, Edward. 'That's my husband, Mr Holmes,' cried Mrs Flowers, close to hysteria. 'Don't you see? Gregory will stop at nothing to get his hands on the money. Using his chemical knowledge, first he poisoned his brother, then his elder nephew. Next it will be Edward, then perhaps even me! At that point, he will be the only member of the immediate family left alive and the entire fortune will be his! You must help, Mr Holmes! Please! I beg you!'

When the lady had recovered from a third bout of weeping, Holmes said he was indeed minded to look into the matter, but would she object if first he asked a few questions?

No, of course not. She was eager to help in any way she could.

To start with, did Mrs Flowers' husband know she had come to see him?

No, he did not. She did not want to alarm him unduly. Not long after he had left for London, shortly before noon, she had waited a quarter of an hour before catching a train to Victoria station and taking a cab directly to Baker Street.

Holmes leaned forwards and wrinkled his nose slightly. Watson records that he knew the movement well: on previous occasions it had indicated that his companion was working to identify a distinctive smell.

Her husband was also in London? Holmes asked.

Yes.

And what time was he expected home?

Probably late. He was not usually back before 8 p.m.

Holmes nodded. And she had no reason to think her husband was in any way unwell?

No, he was in excellent health. They both took regular walks, drank little, and had never smoked.

And Wincott's death ... had she herself set eyes on the scene?

Yes, unfortunately she had. Wincott had also lived in Tunbridge Wells and his maid had summoned her master's brother and wife the moment she discovered the body. As it was a Sunday, they were both at home and Mrs Flowers had entered the room alongside her husband.

And she had no reason to believe the maid had moved the body?

None whatsoever.

Could she describe the scene, as carefully as possible?

Certainly. The dining table, laid for one, was in the centre of the room. Wincott's body was still in a chair, opposite the door, his head and shoulders slumped forwards on to the empty plate before him. The wine glass was on the left ...

Left of what?

Not on our left but on the left of poor Wincott. Stage left, so to speak.

Isn't that unusual? Glasses are usually placed on the right, where they are more easily picked up.

Wincott was left-handed.

The conversation continued for another five minutes, at the end of which Holmes thanked Mrs Flowers for answering his questions so accurately and said he would certainly take on her case.

She thanked him most warmly, bidding him waste not a moment lest Gregory strike before he could be apprehended. Repeating her heartfelt thanks, and warning that her husband was in dire peril, she hastened from the room to be home before Edward's return.

Watson, having agreed to travel to Tunbridge Wells with Holmes the following afternoon, left the Baker Street apartment as the detective was resuming his watch at the window for the elusive Irregular.

The two men met at Victoria station at 2 p.m. the next day. As they were waiting for their train, Holmes bought an early edition of the evening paper and ran an eye over its contents. A short announcement in the 'Stop Press' column caught his eye: the young lawyer, Mr Edward Flowers of Tunbridge Wells, had been found dead at his desk in the office of Simkins and Warburton, 123 The Strand, London.

'Confound the woman,' muttered Holmes. 'She acted sooner than I anticipated.'

Watson was dumbfounded. 'You don't mean to tell me, Holmes,' he exclaimed, 'that you suspect that poor woman of having done away with her own husband?'

'I most certainly do,' Holmes replied. 'I had my suspicions about her from the very start.'

Why?

THE CASE OF THE ENAMEL BROOCH

At the beginning of 'The Adventure of the Veiled Lodger', Watson talks of 'the mass of material' at his command and how his problem was 'not to find but to choose'. As we worked our way through his voluminous notes, we tried to figure out his motives for writing up some into full stories while discarding others. In most instances, the reasons for rejection were obvious: many cases were too similar, or too easily solved. A large number of these he had labelled ROM. We soon deciphered this as Run of the Mill.

Watson used two other acronyms: OPT and PS. One or other of these was scrawled on the jottings pertaining to some thirty cases stored separately from the others in a stout metal box secured with thick cord. The knot had been sealed with wax. A label was attached bearing the following inscription in large letters: SECRET AND HIGHLY

CONFIDENTIAL. Underneath, in smaller freehand, someone had added *Burn rather than make public*.

You can imagine our excitement as we opened the box and lifted out the bundles of dry, crackling paper. Here, at last, were those cases that Watson had alluded to in the opening paragraph of 'The Adventure of the Veiled Lodger': 'The discretion and high sense of professional honour which have always distinguished my friend are still at work in the choice of these memoirs, and no confidence will be abused.' It took no more than a cursory glance to understand what Watson meant: the cases were, without exception, utterly fascinating; half a dozen, at least, were downright scandalous, and not one had made its way into a published collection.

The meaning of OPT became apparent as we read through the top two cases more carefully. The doctor lived for the most part during the reign of Queen Victoria, when matters of a sexual nature were either swept under the carpet or alluded to in the most oblique manner. Though Watson himself was of a liberal persuasion, he was not prepared to offend his readers by going against the social norms of the day. OPT, we deduced, meant Offensive to Public Taste.

It was when we reached the third folder in the pile, the one Watson somewhat coyly entitled 'The Case of the Enamel Brooch', that we guessed the meaning of PS. If Watson's notes are to be believed, it could be only one thing: Politically Sensitive. Whether the case still is, we leave it to you to judge.

Watson was a little surprised when Holmes agreed to take up the case of the enamel brooch. The great detective was not normally susceptible to female charms; indeed, one sometimes gets the impression that he was fonder of his ragamuffin Baker Street Irregulars than of the elegant ladies who came begging his assistance. Yet when Emily de Chablis arrived at 221B Baker Street one sunny July afternoon in 1900, he appeared to allow himself to be swayed by her undoubted attractiveness and agreed to listen to her story.

The young lady made as great an impression on Watson as she had on the detective, and his usually terse notes blossomed into a full description.

Miss de Chablis was of less than average height, though what she lacked in stature she made up for with her vigorous, frank and open manner. Her eyes were bright sapphire, full of vitality, and contrasted strikingly with dark brown hair that framed a somewhat round face that in repose might have looked quite plain, except that she never was in repose. Whether addressing my companion or listening to his replies, she was all energy, cocking her head like a sparrow and continually fidgeting her short fingers.

However, it was not the lady's mannerisms that held my attention so much as her doll-like appearance. She reminded me of a very well-known personage, though at the time I could not for the life of me recall who it was.

Miss de Chablis' request was of the mundane sort that rarely inspired Holmes to engage his considerable intellect, and Watson writes how Holmes would normally have dismissed the client politely but perfunctorily after a few lines of conversation. The lady was seeking the detective's help in tracing her parentage. From Dickens onwards, writers and historians have pointed out that the much-vaunted Victorian 'respectability' thinly disguised the churning sordidness of a society in which probably half the population was born out of wedlock and a further quarter had no idea who their father – and perhaps even their mother – was. So, for Holmes, what set Miss de Chablis apart from the others?

She had come at the request of her fiancé, Frank Goresby-Jones, a respectable young doctor from Kidderminster. Watson's notes are not very full on the background to the story, but it seems that Dr Goresby-Jones's father was a Methodist minister of some repute and, before solemnizing his son's marriage to Miss de Chablis, he wished to reassure himself of the respectability of what he called her 'heritage'. The girl's mother, Liza, had died shortly after giving birth, leaving the child to be brought up by her aunt, Mrs Mitcham. The aunt's family – her husband and five children, all older than Emily – passed the Reverend Goresby-Jones's respectability test with flying colours. But one or two question marks remained over their adopted relative.

Emily knew only what her aunt had told her. Her mother, the headstrong Miss Liza Wilkins, had gone to Paris at the age of twenty-one to take up a position as an English teacher in a private school for young ladies. From there she wrote to announce that she had fallen in love with and married Édouard de Chablis, a Frenchman from an old and distinguished family. The Mitchams were surprised – even a little shocked – by the announcement, as they had never met M. de Chablis, nor had Liza talked much about him in her infrequent letters.

The story took a tragic turn when, one rainy evening in November 1882, a heavily pregnant and much distressed Mme de Chablis appeared on her sister's doorstep to announce that her husband had been murdered, leaving her a penniless widow. Emily was born ten days later, and her mother died of a haemorrhage two days after the birth.

In accordance with her future father-in-law's wishes, the eighteen-year-old Emily had questioned her aunt about her parents but had learned nothing more than she already knew: her mother, Miss Liza Wilkins, had been an English teacher in Paris, and Emily's father was the older brother of one of Liza's pupils. Quite how or why he had died, Mrs Mitcham had no idea, and short of going to Paris and searching the newspapers for reports of his murder, there was no way Emily could find out.

Having heard Miss de Chablis' story, Holmes 'studied

her very closely, to the point where the young lady blushed and turned away, declaring that she did not care to be examined as if she were a racehorse'. Holmes apologized but insisted that his behaviour was necessary if he were to help her. He then asked whether she had any of her mother's possessions. 'Just one,' the girl had replied. She took from her handbag a blue, heart-shaped enamel brooch, set in gold, and handed it to the detective.

Holmes's eyes 'lit up like beacons' the moment he beheld the item. After examining it carefully for a few moments, he passed it over to Watson. The doctor recorded that it was 'sizeable and very well made, and probably of considerable value'. Embedded into the enamel was the word 'Edward' and, beneath, the phrase 'du Chab'.

Watson assumed, as did Emily, that the brooch had been given to Liza by her husband, using the English form of his name ('Edward' for 'Édouard') and abbreviating his surname to 'du Chab'. After his client had gone, Holmes would explain to Watson that this 'series of entirely logical deductions' was 'patently false'. But at the time he simply gave a wry smile and told his client she could assure her future father-in-law that her heritage was not only respectable, but 'a good deal more respectable than that of any Methodist minister in the kingdom'.

On what grounds did he feel able to make such a statement?

THE MYSTERY OF THE FOURTH TROMBONE

As you may recall, Sherlock Holmes was an enthusiastic musician who played the solo violin and went to the occasional concert. It was his attendance at one of the Albert Hall's popular Sunday afternoon concerts that drew him into what his friend Watson would later label 'The Mystery of the Fourth Trombone'.

Watson's notes tell us that Holmes had a strong disinclination to be recognized in public. This was partly due to an innate dislike of trivial social intercourse, partly because professionally it suited him to be as unrecognizable as possible, and partly because – after the incident of Mrs Arbuthnot's Siamese – he was loath to get involved in matters that did not interest him. (Mrs Sylvia Arbuthnot, the aunt of a young man Holmes had assisted, recognized him while he was walking down Regent Street and pleaded with him in a very loud voice for a quarter of an hour to help find her missing cat.) Consequently, Holmes and Watson booked a box at the Albert Hall to enjoy the concert in relative privacy.

We are told only about the second half of the concert, which comprised two works. The first was Arthur Sullivan's *The Golden Legend*, a sentimental cantata that Holmes appeared to enjoy. The second he dismissed as 'a vulgar noise, a shameful and cheap episode of nationalistic bombast', and proposed they leave before it was played. Watson objected and, for once, Holmes gave way, reluctantly agreeing to sit through Tchaikovsky's *1812 Overture*.

There was a short interval while the choir left the stage and some of the Imperial Symphony Orchestra took a quick break after the Sullivan work. As they returned to take their places for the overture, Watson noticed a change in his friend's demeanour. Holmes's face tensed and he leaned forwards, staring at the players. When Watson asked what the matter was, Holmes pointed a long, bony finger at the brass section.

'Fourth trombone's missing,' he said. 'Went off after the Sullivan and hasn't reappeared. Strange, Watson. Maybe the poor fellow's been taken ill. I would have thought they'd want all the brassy cacophony they could muster for the *Sturm und Drang* you've press-ganged me into enduring next.'

The other trombonists' baffled glances and discreet shrugs intimated that they shared Holmes's puzzlement. Watson, who failed to notice this, put his friend's agitation over the missing musician down to his being obliged to stay for a piece he did not enjoy. After a few more grumpy remarks, Holmes settled down. Oskar Horváth, the Hungarian-born conductor, came back on to his rostrum, bowed to the audience amid loud applause, placed his pocket watch before him on the lectern, opened the score, raised his arms … and the orchestra glided into the ominous opening bars of the famous overture.

At first, all went well. Though Holmes was clearly not enjoying the music, he sat still and silent. But after a couple of minutes, his agitation returned. Whereas he had previously praised Horváth and the orchestra's harmonious playing, he was now frowning and beating time with his fingers in an irritated manner.

Watson signalled him to desist. Holmes shook his head. 'Fellow's lost his sense of tempo,' he whispered.

Watson turned back towards the orchestra. To him, Horváth certainly appeared more animated than before, continually glancing down at the lectern and waving his arms to mark the beat with exaggerated clarity. Subtle glances between members of the orchestra suggested they, too, sensed all was not as it should be.

The eccentric behaviour and tiny irregularities were noticed only by practised musicians, and the maestro successfully steered the overture to its celebrated bell-ringing, cannon-firing conclusion. The vigour of the percussion section made up for the lack of real guns, and the audience roared their approval even as the final note was still reverberating around the auditorium. Holmes shrugged and shouted over the din that it was a pity to conclude a pleasant afternoon with such vulgarity.

'Like a thunderstorm at the end of a picnic,' suggested Watson.

'Though I have never taken a picnic,' said Holmes, 'I should think that a most fitting analogy.'

Storm clouds reappeared the following morning when Watson read out a newspaper report stating that, around 6.30 p.m. the previous evening, Charles de Mainville, the

fourth trombone of the Imperial Symphony Orchestra, had been found dead in the Gentlemen's lavatory of the Albert Hall's Green Room. Though he had been violently sick, that was not the cause of death. He had died of a single bullet wound to the head, and a pistol lay on the floor beside the body. The police did not suspect foul play.

'Apparently been dead for no more than an hour,' noted Watson. 'How sad! He must have shot himself towards the end of the Tchaikovsky. With all that mock cannon fire, no wonder we didn't hear the gun.'

'Half right!' retorted Holmes, springing to his feet. 'Come on, Watson! We must get down to the Yard and instruct the dunderheads in blue to consider a murder investigation. And they would do well to begin by questioning Oskar Horváth.'

Why on earth did Holmes believe the conductor had played a part in the death of the fourth trombone?

THE MYSTERY OF THE STRANGLED POET

The great majority of Sherlock Holmes's cases written up by his friend Watson concerned – to put it bluntly – sex and violence. The violence was usually murder, often gruesome. 'Sex' covered a multitude of sins (and other matters), ranging from clandestine affairs, 'illegitimate' births, and other behaviour considered immoral by the standards of the day. Watson, a man of liberal views, was happy to write up such tales as long as he did not think they would offend his readers. Only a few cases featured issues that were so OPT (Offensive to Public Taste) that he never dared bring them before the public. One of these was 'The Mystery of the Strangled Poet'.

The case centred upon the murder of Tertius Fawcett, a twenty-six-year-old English master and resident house tutor at Appleford College. This minor public school for boys, founded in 1551, occupied the site of a Benedictine Abbey on the Dorset coast. It described itself as 'traditional, in the very best sense of the word', and attracted the sons of local farmers and tradesmen, together with those of more illustrious parents whose offspring had failed to find a place in one of the better-known public schools.

It was one of these illustrious parents, Lord Abbas, who called on Holmes in his Baker Street lodgings at about 11 o'clock on a raw morning in early February and demanded in a most forceful manner that the detective put a stop to the 'scurrilous and wholly unfounded rumours' that were circulating about him. Holmes politely pointed out that he needed to hear the details of the case before he could decide whether or not to take it on.

Lord Abbas huffed and puffed and muttered a few disparaging remarks about 'upstarts' before eventually telling his story. His thirteen-year-old son, the Honourable Edward Romsey-Ffolkes, was a first-year pupil in Cranmer House, Appleford College. He was, the peer admitted, 'rather a pretty boy, with more of his mother in his looks than was good for him'. This became apparent when Edward's beauty caught the attention of Tertius Fawcett.

Frequently – as many as five times a week – Fawcett had invited Edward into his rooms in the evening to assist him with his homework (known as 'prep'). The conversations between the tutor and the boy became more and more intimate until – according to Lord Abbas – 'Fawcett put

his filthy hand on my boy's knee and said that, in the finest tradition of the ancient Greeks, he loved him.'

The peer got to hear of 'the Fawcett incident' during the Christmas holidays, when the boy casually mentioned it to his mother among a string of other 'amusing things' that had happened to him during the Michaelmas term. Incensed, Lord Abbas had immediately demanded an interview with Dr Abercrombie Middleton, Appleford College's mild-mannered, academic headmaster.

The meeting did not go well. Dr Middleton, a classical scholar, appeared to find the tutor's behaviour more interesting than scandalous. He had, he said, often wondered about the nature of the relationship between men and boys in ancient Greece. Nevertheless, he would have a quiet word with Fawcett, advising him to 'temper his favouritism towards the prettier young boys in his house'.

At this, Lord Abbas confessed to having 'exploded with fury'. Dr Middleton's 'limp response' was 'wholly inadequate', he had thundered in a voice clearly audible to the headmaster's secretary and the Head of History, who were conversing in an adjacent room. A 'quiet word' was no way to deal with the sort of lewd advances his young son had been subjected to, the peer continued. Speaking even louder than before, he said Fawcett should be horsewhipped and dismissed from the school. If the 'dirty-minded fop' were still in position during the Lent term, his lordship swore that 'he could not be held responsible for what might happen'. Asked by Holmes if those were the exact words he had used, the peer acknowledged that they were. He regretted it, for now they had come back to haunt him.

Tertius Fawcett was not dismissed from his post and, after a 'quiet word' from the headmaster, he continued to teach English literature – and assist the Honourable Edward Romsey-Ffolkes with his prep. But not for long. On 1 February, just three weeks into the Lent term, the young master was found strangled in his study.

As there was no obvious suspect, the story of the peer's outburst raised considerable suspicion. He had enough common sense to understand why. He agreed that he had a motive for wishing Fawcett harm, and his veiled threat, intended to force the headmaster into dismissing the man,

63

could be interpreted as suggesting violence. But it was a gross injustice for his life to be made intolerable because a few ill-judged remarks spoken in anger had been overheard by 'a pair of gossiping old pedants'.

'I didn't have anything to do with the wretched man's murder,' his lordship concluded, 'and I would be most grateful, Mr Holmes, if you would come down to Dorset, find out who the killer is, and clear my name. Good God! Even my own tenants look at me with suspicion!'

When Lord Abbas had finished, Sherlock Holmes sat in silence for a few moments before declaring that the case was sufficiently interesting to merit his attention. If his lordship was prepared to pay the required fee without receiving a guarantee that his name would be cleared, the detective would take the 09.13 from Waterloo to Dorchester the next morning. The peer agreed, wrote out a cheque for the first half of Holmes's fee, and showed himself out.

On arriving at Dorchester, Holmes went to the headquarters of the Dorset Constabulary and introduced himself to Detective Sergeant Granger, the young officer handling the Fawcett murder. Painfully caught between the search for truth and the fury of a local grandee, Granger warmly welcomed Holmes's assistance. He confirmed the accuracy of the story related by Lord Abbas in Baker Street, and handed over the evidence he had gathered during his investigations.

The night of the murder had been a particularly stormy one, with a fierce gale from the south-west. Despite this, one of the casements of Fawcett's bay window was found to have been open all night. Granger had discovered no footprints or other marks in the soil of the flowerbed immediately beneath the open casement. The housemaster of Cranmer House said that, to the best of his knowledge, all external doors to the building had been locked from the inside.

Granger had questioned a dozen Cranmer boys. Most said they liked but did not respect their tutor, whom they nicknamed 'Fondler Fawcett'. He was an eccentric young man, never locking the door to his rooms and leaving his study window permanently open to 'cool his fevered heart'. The nature of that fever was confirmed by the erotic prints found hidden between the pages of a volume of Oscar Wilde's poetry: images of acts that would, in Watson's words, 'have brought blushes to the cheeks of the most brazen, and sent the perpetrators to jail for many years'.

Fawcett's body was found after breakfast by a boy seeking advice about his part in the house play. The doctor who examined the corpse said it had lain there for between six and eight hours, meaning the tutor was killed in the early hours of the morning. He had been strangled with the bare hands of a very strong person, almost certainly a man. As there were no signs of a struggle, Granger deduced that either the tutor was taken by surprise or his assailant was known to him.

Fawcett had poetic aspirations, Granger said, and had been working on a piece the very night he was killed. 'It seems to have been inspired by that night's storm,' the young detective suggested as he handed Holmes a sheet of paper. On it, amid several blotches, were just four lines:

> *The storm that rages up above,*
> *What has this to do with love?*
> *The time has come! Enough! No more!*
> *I must betray what I abhor.*

Holmes read it, nodded, and handed back the paper.

Having given Holmes all the evidence he had mustered, Granger confessed to being 'stumped'. The obvious culprit was Lord Abbas. But the peer swore that on the night in question he had been at home in Compton Hall. His wife, a thin, timid lady, confirmed that as far as she knew this was correct. She and Lord Abbas had separate bedrooms, and she had retired early, leaving her husband drinking alone. The butler remembered bringing his lordship a bottle of port at about half-past ten and then going to bed. The stable boy had not heard anyone leaving or arriving during the night. When he fed the horses the next morning, none of them showed any sign of having been ridden for at least twenty-four hours.

Even if Lord Abbas had managed to sneak out of his house and ride to Appleford, Granger explained, it was well-nigh impossible that he, or an assassin hired by him, could have entered Cranmer House, committed the murder, and made good their escape without being seen or leaving a trace of their presence. To this observation, Sherlock Holmes made no comment.

Holmes ate a light lunch and drove to Appleford College in a hired dog cart. He arrived in the middle of the afternoon and made a quick survey of the campus before announcing himself. Cranmer House, an ancient, E-shaped structure, stood on a promontory some 200 yards south-west of the other college buildings.

The boys' dormitory was on the first floor of the long down-stroke of the E, facing directly on to the sea and the frequent south-westerly gales. Three annexes formed the prongs of the E. Situated on the more sheltered side of the building, they overlooked the rest of the college and their houses. From north to south they were: the rooms of the house tutor and resident matron, the kitchens, and the housemaster's quarters. Fawcett's rooms were on the ground floor, immediately below the matron's. The stone-mullioned bay window of his study looked over flowerbeds and lawns to the restored monastic church that served as a place of worship for both the college and the local parish.

Having completed his survey, Holmes made his way to the main school building and was shown into the headmaster's study. Dr Middleton welcomed him warmly and hoped he would be able to 'sort out the whole unsatisfactory business as swiftly as possible'. He had nothing further to add to the information he had already given to Granger, all of which was already in Holmes's possession.

Holmes then made his way to Cranmer House. He was greeted by the housemaster, Mr Montague Wray, who showed him around and went over the events of the night of the murder once more. His account tallied in every way with that related by Granger and by the headmaster. On hearing from Lord Abbas the previous evening that Holmes was on the case, Wray had been delighted: the scandal was doing the reputation of the school, and his house in particular, no good whatsoever.

When asked for his opinion of Fawcett, Wray confessed that, though he was devastated by what had happened, the tutor had not been his type. He was too foppish for Cranmer. Wray's was a sporty house that prided itself on turning boys into men capable of ruling the Empire. It was a tough, 'surnames only' place. Crawley, his Head of House, was the epitome of a 'Cranmer man': Head of School as well as Head of House, captain of the first-XV rugby team, and bright enough to be destined for Oxford. He was a bit of a brute on the rugby field and occasionally let his temper get the better of him, but all in all he was 'a first-rate chap, absolutely first rate'.

Holmes said he looked forward to meeting the young man. Meanwhile, would Wray tell him precisely what he had been doing on the night of the murder?

The housemaster said he had made a quick tour of the house just before 11 p.m. – he was sure of the time because he heard the church clock strike the hour as he shut the door to his apartment and joined Mrs Wray in their sitting room. On his rounds he had made sure all the boys were in bed and the door to the kitchen was locked.

Had Wray checked the external doors?

No, it was the Head of House's responsibility to see they were securely fastened at lights-out time, 10.30 p.m.

Where was Crawley when the housemaster made his rounds?

He was in bed in his cubicle at the southern end of the dormitory.

Was he asleep?

He appeared to be, yes.

Finally, had Wray seen Fawcett that evening?

No, but he remembered seeing a light beneath his door as he passed by on his rounds.

Holmes thanked Wray for his help and asked to speak to the matron. Wray said she had taken the day off at short notice to visit her sick sister in Weymouth, but should have returned by now. His surmise was correct. Holmes found Mrs Sophia Mussett, an attractive woman of around thirty years of age, still in the cloak and bonnet she had worn for her journey. A little flustered by the sudden appearance of so distinguished a visitor, she bade Holmes take a seat while she put away her things and tidied herself.

Mrs Mussett had decorated her parlour, which also served as her surgery, with a variety of school memorabilia, including a framed photograph of the House rugby team. Five years previously, she explained when she came back into the room, her husband had been killed in Africa. Widowed and destitute, she had lived with her sister in Weymouth before accepting the post at Cranmer. It was, she said, the best thing she could have done. She loved every minute of her time here.

Holmes questioned her about the precise nature of her duties and asked to see the book in which she kept a record of the boys who came to her evening surgeries. Among the sprained ankles, chilblains and other ailments listed on the night of Fawcett's murder, Holmes noted 'Sebastian Crawley' next to the word 'heartburn'.

Yes, Mrs Mussett smiled, Sebastian had called in to ask whether she had any medicine for indigestion. She had given him a spoonful of Hepar sulph, as recommended by Mrs Beeton.

Crawley's name appeared quite frequently in her surgery book, Holmes observed. Was he sickly?

Mrs Mussett laughed. Sickly? No. Sebastian was the fittest boy in the house. His visits had all been related to injuries sustained on the rugby field.

Did Mrs Mussett know Mr Fawcett well?

No, she rarely spoke to him.

Had she heard of the incident involving Lord Abbas's son?

Indeed she had, and in her opinion the headmaster should have sacked Fawcett on the spot. He was a disgusting young man who had made no secret of his dislike of women.

Holmes thanked her for her honesty and returned to the housemaster's study. He had just one final interview to conduct. Could someone be sent to find Crawley? A junior boy was duly dispatched and ten minutes later the Head of School entered the room. Over six foot tall, broad-shouldered, and blessed with the steady eye of a sportsman, he was every inch as impressive as Wray had made out.

Had he liked Mr Fawcett, Holmes asked?

No sir, replied the Adonis. He had respected the man's scholarship but disliked his unmanly ways. He had found the business with Edward Romsey-Ffolkes despicable. Fawcett certainly wasn't a gentleman, Crawley continued. In class the young master used to make disparaging remarks about women, including Mrs Mussett and the housemaster's wife, Mrs Wray.

Could Crawley explain what he meant by 'disparaging remarks'? The young man hesitated and a faint blush came into his cheek. He had heard Fawcett refer to both ladies as 'Delilahs'.

Where had Crawley been on the night of the murder?

In bed in his cubicle in the dormitory.

Had he been asleep when Mr Wray did his rounds?

No, he had lain awake for a long time listening to the wind and thinking of team selection for the next match. The last thing he remembered was hearing the church clock strike half-past twelve.

The final interview concluded, Holmes bade farewell to Mr Wray and returned to the Abbas Arms, where he had booked a room. The next morning, he travelled back to Dorchester and called in on Granger. A careful search of the matron's rooms in Cranmer House, he suggested, would almost certainly reveal valuable new evidence leading to the arrest of Fawcett's murderer.

Granger did as Holmes suggested and an arrest was made the same afternoon.

Who was arrested on suspicion of murder, and on what evidence?

The Adventure of the Axelbury Arsonist

In 'The Adventure of the Cardboard Box', Watson reminds us that Sherlock Holmes took no great interest in the natural world, for 'neither the country nor the sea presented the slightest attraction to him'. He was never truly happy unless in London, lying 'in the very centre of five millions of people'. It was with some reluctance, therefore, that in the spring of 1907 he agreed to travel down to Somerset to take up what appeared to be a very ordinary case of arson.

There had been a lull in the usual activities of 221B Baker Street when Holmes had received a short letter, written in a large, confident, female hand, begging him to visit Axelbury Hall, Nether Stowey, and 'sort out a wretched case of beastly fire-raising'. The author of the letter ended by offering to pay 'any fee, or royalty or whatever-you-call-it, plus expenses, etc., etc., etc.'. Pecuniary reward, though welcome to Holmes, meant less to him than the chance to

exercise his formidable powers in the furtherance of justice, and he would normally have dismissed such hysterical pleading. But the extravagant signature at the bottom of the one-page epistle convinced him otherwise.

Miss Agatha Teasebury, the 'Dove of Drury Lane', was an actress whose beauty had once turned the head of every young man in London, including that of the young bachelor, John H. Watson. Now a widower, the doctor recorded that he was 'desperately eager to set eyes on one who had illuminated the London stage for so many years', and Holmes, in a rare fit of kindness, acceded to his colleague's quixotic wish.

The detective's decision was also influenced by a more professional matter. Shortly after Christmas the previous year, a thief had robbed Miss Teasebury of a diamond and pearl necklace valued at over £100,000. It had never been recovered. Holmes was presented with the unusual opportunity of solving two mysteries at the same time, although he admitted privately to Watson that it was the missing necklace that held the greater allure for him.

Before exchanging the buzz of the city for the bucolic snores of Somerset, Holmes mined his scrapbooks to remind himself of the facts of the Teasebury robbery. The burglar had apparently entered the Hall one evening while the actress was entertaining guests in the dining room. As all the doors were unlocked and the staff busy with the dinner party, he (and it was almost certainly a man) had simply walked in, made his way straight to the actress's bedroom, rifled through her dressing table, found the necklace, and walked out with it.

No one saw the intruder until Miss Teasebury's chauffeur, George Hazelhurst, spotted a stranger standing next to his mistress's motor car, which was parked to one side of the Hall. The chauffeur said the man looked as if he had been there a few minutes and was trying to get the motor started, probably to use for his getaway. When challenged, the man remained beside the motor car for a moment, then ran off before Hazelhurst could get a good look at him.

Piccard Grantham, a crab fisherman from Minehead who had lost his boat in a recent storm, was apprehended shortly afterwards for another robbery, and was now behind the bars of Shepton Mallet prison. Though the chauffeur said Grantham looked very like the figure he had seen beside the motor, Grantham denied all knowledge of the Teasebury necklace and the jewel was never recovered.

Actresses, even the most celebrated, rarely accumulate great fortunes through their talent alone. So it was with Agatha Teasebury. As she approached her fiftieth birthday, she had married Adolphus Grinkwaller III, an American entrepreneur who had made a vast fortune in mining and steel. Miss Teasebury had agreed to join him at the altar on condition that he settled in England, within reasonable reach of London. The millionaire duly obliged by acquiring Axelbury Hall, near Nether Stowey, and its surrounding 1,750-acre estate of farms and deer parks.

Sadly, Mr Grinkwaller did not enjoy his position within the ranks of the English landed gentry for long. Six months after his marriage, he fell from his horse while out with the Quantock Staghounds and died of a broken neck. Agatha responded with a theatrically broken heart.

Miss Teasebury's breakage proved less permanent than her husband's, and she soon settled into a quiet life in the country, punctuated by occasional guest appearances on the London stage. Her resident household comprised three maids, a cook, a butler, a housekeeper, and a chauffeur. She refused to have anything to do with horses after her husband's death, choosing instead to be driven to Taunton station in the splendid scarlet Buick her husband had brought over from the United States.

It was the loss of this motor car, the one that the intruder had supposedly been trying to start, that had prompted Miss Teasebury to write to Sherlock Holmes.

The cab driver who collected the detective and his friend at Taunton station revealed that over the past three weeks there had been five cases of arson in and around the Quantock Hills. He didn't know about the latest, the destruction of the Teasebury Buick, but the first four had all been started in the same manner. A hay bale was placed next to the garage doors, doused in lamp oil, and set alight. By the time the fire brigade arrived, the flames had burned through the wooden doors and destroyed the car within.

Fortunately, there had been no major casualties, though a stable boy sleeping in a loft above one of the vehicles had been lucky to escape with only minor burns. The police were looking for a male or female whose livelihood was threatened by the expansion of the motor car at the expense of horse-drawn vehicles. There were several suspects but not yet sufficient evidence to apprehend anyone.

Having booked themselves into a nearby coaching inn, Holmes and Watson presented themselves at Axelbury Hall. The doctor found the Dove of Drury Lane 'every bit as magnificent at close quarters as she was on the stage'. Clearly smitten, he drew on Shakespeare to express his wonder. 'Age cannot wither her,' he wrote in his notes, 'nor custom stale her infinite variety.' Unsurprisingly, Holmes was not similarly bowled over, and said he pronounced the comparison between Agatha Teasebury and Cleopatra 'a little far-fetched'.

The Buick had been housed in a stone garage set in a copse some fifty yards to the west of the Hall. The chauffeur's cottage, similarly stone-built, stood ten yards away on the edge of the trees. The garage walls had survived the blaze, but the wooden doors and roof were utterly destroyed, and the vehicle within had been reduced to a blackened skeleton of twisted metal.

Holmes examined the wreckage in the company of the chauffeur. The poor man admitted to being overcome with grief and guilt at having allowed the destruction of a possession that meant so much to his mistress.

Holmes looked at him sharply. 'Guilt?'

Hazelhurst sheepishly stooped to pick up the padlock used to secure the garage doors. It was open.

Holmes nodded. 'And only you had a key?' he asked.

'I'm the only one as uses it, sir. It hangs on a nail inside the servants' entrance. It's still there, I reckon. I could have sworn I'd locked up secure, but I am a bit careless sometimes. Obviously, I didn't close the padlock properly after the last time I took the motor out.'

'Obviously. And when was the last time?'

'Only two days ago, sir. I went over to Shepton Mallet to collect a spare tyre from Armstrong Motors. You can see what's left of it up against the wall there.' He indicated a circle of charred rubber.

'You went alone?'

'No, sir. I took the maid, Molly Fish, with me. She needed to buy clothing. I didn't enquire too closely, sir, as I believe it was something, you know, female.'

'And she returned with you?'

'Yes, sir. I had to wait a while for her because she said her bloom … I mean her clothes … were not quite ready.' Hazelhurst coughed and glanced up anxiously.

'Yes?'

'Well, I know it's only gossip, sir, but I've heard the ladies say Molly has a young man, secret-like. Perhaps she may have been a bit late because she was meeting him. She did look a touch flustered …'

'Thank you, Hazelhurst. That's enough of the gossip. Back to the facts. Did Molly accompany you on previous trips to Armstrong Motors?'

'Only once, sir. A month back. I had to collect a pump, and she had volunteered to pick up linen for the guest bedrooms.'

Holmes nodded and, after pausing a moment to reflect on what he had heard, began examining the remains of the car. Hazelhurst stood beside Watson, twisting his cap nervously between his fingers.

A couple of minutes later, Holmes uttered a small cry of surprise. Although he couldn't be certain, it looked as if the car's petrol tank had been cut open with a hacksaw.

Hazelhurst approached to take a closer look. 'Well I'll

be blowed, sir!' he muttered, stooping over the wreckage. 'Looks as if the villain really wanted to make sure this one went up – cut open the petrol tank so the flames would be sure to reach the fuel.'

Holmes stood up. 'Yes, very likely. Do you have a hacksaw, Hazelhurst?'

'I did, sir.' He pointed to the charred remains of a wooden toolbox. 'Looks as if I've lost my tools as well as my motor car.'

'One last question, Hazelhurst.'

'Yes, sir?'

'Do you think it possible that the blaze was started outside the garage doors, then spread inside once they were alight?'

'No, sir. When I arrived, the doors were still burning – from the inside.'

'Thank you, Hazelhurst. Most illuminating.'

The following morning Watson hired a pony and trap, and, in the company of the local police constable, he and Holmes toured the other four arson sites. Two had already been cleared up, but at the others the detective was able to make a thorough examination of the wreckage. After lunching in Crowcombe, the party returned in the rain over the hills to the Hall.

By now Holmes was sniffing loudly and often. It was, warned Watson, a sure sign that his friend had caught a cold by dashing about on the Quantocks in the rain. Holmes frowned, sniffed again, and said he knew he should have stayed in London. Nevertheless, he would continue his investigation. With Miss Teasebury's permission, he would like to interview all her employees in their living quarters. After delighting Watson – but irritating Holmes – with a story about an admirer forcing his way into her dressing room 'without so much as a knock at the door', she consented to the detective starting his interviews.

He began with the chauffeur in his cottage and ended with Molly in her quarters at the top of the house. While there, his cold appeared to get worse and he sat sniffing like a steam engine as she answered his questions.

When the process was over, Holmes, finding the Hall was not on the telephone network, took the housekeeper's dog cart into Nether Stowey to make a call. He returned half an hour later in the company of the local constable.

'We have had a pleasant and most successful couple of days, Watson,' he declared, now completely free of the symptoms of the cold that had dogged him earlier. 'I will leave my good friend Constable Diggins to arrest the villain who destroyed that magnificent motor car. And at the same time, he will return the Teasebury necklace to its rightful owner. But we, my dear friend, must hurry away or we will miss the last train back to London.'

During their journey, Holmes explained to Watson how he discovered who had set fire to the Buick and how the arson was related to the recovery of the Teasebury necklace. In a single visit, he had achieved his aim of identifying the arsonist *and* solving the mystery of the missing necklace.

What did he say to Watson?

The Mystery of the Early Cuckoo

A s electricity gradually replaced gas as the chosen form of lighting in the houses of the wealthy, a number of intriguing gadgets were produced for those with a reliable electricity supply. One of these was the Sauber Electric Cuckoo Clock (patent applied for), designed and constructed in Birmingham by Gustav Strauss.

Holmes had admired some of these ingenious timepieces in the homes of his well-heeled clients, and he read with interest the *Daily Telegraph*'s report of the inventor's unfortunate death. Mr Strauss had been found dead in his bath, electrocuted by one of his own clocks.

The following day Holmes received an unannounced visit from the clockmaker's widow. Though the police refused to believe her, Mrs Strauss was convinced that her husband's death had not been an accident. Holmes was intrigued and asked her to explain her reasoning.

Mrs Lilly Strauss, a handsome, down-to-earth woman of around forty, told her story with admirable clarity. She began with a personal confession: she and Gustav had never married. Though they lived as man and wife and had three lovely children, in the eyes of the law they had always been Mr Gustav Strauss and Miss Lilly Phillips.

The decision not to marry had been Gustav's. He assured Lilly it was not because he already had a wife, but because, as a modern man of science, he had no time for 'customs and rituals left over from the age of superstition'. As Lilly was neither a church nor a chapel woman, she was happy to go along with her partner's wish.

The couple had met shortly after Gustav had moved from Switzerland to Birmingham, where he had opened the workshop that manufactured the now famous Sauber Electric Cuckoo Clock. Why Sauber and not Strauss? Sauber was his mother's maiden name, he said, and he had named the clock after her as a tribute. His father had died when he was six and his mother ten years later. He was the only offspring of their union.

Though not a formalized marriage, the relationship between Gustav and Lilly was easy enough. As the number of houses wired for electricity multiplied, so demand for the novelty cuckoo clock grew and Strauss became a wealthy man. He and Lilly bought a substantial new villa in a leafy suburb, took on a cook and a housemaid, and paid for their children to be privately educated. The success of the clock even attracted the attention of the press when the *Illustrated London News* made it and its inventor the subject of an article entitled 'A New Man of the Electric Age'.

It was shortly after the publication of this article that the first of a series of unsettling issues arose. Letters from abroad started appearing, addressed to a 'Mr Sauber-Strauss'. Gustav dismissed them as enquiries from a confused civil servant in Bern asking about a property bequeathed by an aunt of his. Unimportant though he said the letters were, he was agitated when they arrived and threw them on the fire after a quick glance at their contents. Lilly, who spoke neither French nor German, did not read them.

Gustav's agitation increased when, in the middle of March, the first cuckoo of spring was heard in the woods opposite their house. The bird was a month early, everyone agreed, and ornithologists scoured the woods for it. The early migrant was never found, and when its call was heard no more, experts said it had probably died of cold. Throughout the whole incident, Gustav had been unusually edgy with his wife and the children.

'It was about then that the itinerant French tinker began working the streets around where we live,' said Lilly. Holmes raised a surprised eyebrow and urged her to continue.

The tinker was an eccentric fellow, Lilly went on, but very amusing. He was painfully short-sighted, lean as a rake, with long hair and a huge bushy beard. Unable to afford spectacles he would go right up close to people and ask them with his strong French accent, 'Pleeze, yu 'av pot I mend?'

The children thought this immensely funny and christened him 'Mr Potamend'! Even Gustav, who at first had treated the fellow with suspicion, was forced to admit that he was 'a bit of a laugh'.

The laughter was short-lived, however. In the first week of April, Lilly and the children went to visit her sister in Darlington. She gave the cook a couple of days off and left the maid in charge of day-to-day household matters. Gustav did not object to her going but asked her not to stay away too long as he did not enjoy being in the house without her. When she returned four days later, she was surprised to find the maid waiting for her on the doorstep. The young woman was hugely apologetic. She had taken the previous evening off, had 'a bit of a tipple' and lost her house key. After staying the night with her friend Dotty, she had tried several times to rouse Mr Strauss to let her back in, but he had not responded. The reason became apparent as soon as Lilly went upstairs and followed an electric cable from the landing into the bathroom.

The accident, the police said, had occurred sometime the previous evening. Mr Strauss had wired up one of his cuckoo clocks and propped it up on the edge of the bath so he could admire it as he washed. He had clearly not set it down securely, concluded the investigating detective, for it had slipped into the water and electrocuted him. The officer had also found the lid of the bureau in the drawing room open, with the key still in the lock. The contents of the desk had been scattered about, but Lilly confirmed nothing had been taken. The detective concluded that Mr Strauss had been searching for something in his bureau before deciding to take a bath.

Lilly was not convinced. First, Gustav was fully aware how dangerous it was to operate electrical machinery near water, she said, and he would never have taken one of his clocks into the bathroom. Second, he never under any circumstances left his bureau unlocked. The key had been taken from the pocket of his dressing gown, where he normally kept it. The garment had been found hanging on a peg inside the bathroom door – the first place an intruder searching for the key might have looked before ransacking the house. Consequently, Lilly was sure someone other than her husband had opened the bureau, presumably looking for something inside.

What had Gustav kept in the bureau? Holmes asked.

Only family and household papers, he was told. All business documents, including accounts, patents and so forth, were held in the Sauber workshop.

Holmes found the lady's story convincing, and went to Birmingham to investigate.

First, he examined the offending cuckoo clock. It was different from all the others he had seen, for it had no maker's name on the face. Lilly, who had not seen it before either, said it was a very early design, probably a hand-made prototype.

Holmes then had a long chat with the maid. She was fortunate not to have been dismissed, she said, as she had made a real fool of herself that night. It was her evening off, and she had gone down to the Brickmaker's Arms with Dotty for a bit of fun. Everyone was there, even that crazy French tinker, and they'd had quite a sing-song. After several glasses of port (she'd forgotten exactly how many), she'd left her handbag with Dotty and gone to the toilet. When she returned, Dotty was dancing on top of a table. It was not until they were preparing to leave that she noticed someone had been at her bag. The thief had taken her house key and the small change from her purse, but, oddly, had not touched a ten-shilling note.

Was the French tinker still in the district? Holmes asked. No, the maid replied. The day after Mr Strauss's death, he had moved to the parish in which the Sauber clock workshop was situated.

That was where Holmes went next. Finding the tinker plying his trade in the market square, he engaged him in conversation. As he was talking, Holmes took small steps backwards and forwards, as if nervous. In fact, he was carefully watching the man's eyes to see if his myopia was as serious as Lilly had told him. He concluded that it was not. He also noticed a fine silver watch chain hanging from an inside pocket of his coat – a strange accoutrement for one who professed himself too poor to afford spectacles.

Holmes, who addressed the man in fluent French, learned he was from Saint-Jean-de-Monts in the west of France. He had found little work in his native Vendée and was now trying his luck in England, 'where the money is'. After a relaxed chat, Holmes bade him farewell, saying that if he came to London he must call on Mrs Hudson, who was sure to have pots that needed mending.

The man gave him a strange look, then a broad grin spread over his face and he replied that he would certainly come and see 'Mr Cottage' (the pseudonym Holmes had been using) if he were ever in London.

Holmes had switched to German when offering his invitation. How did a tinker born and bred in the Vendée, he asked, know enough German to understand Mr Cottage's questions and reply in the same language? Ah! the man replied. After leaving home he had spent five years in Hamburg before coming to Birmingham.

Stranger and stranger, thought Holmes. He had delivered his parting invitation in *Schweizerdeutsch* (Swiss-German), a dialect the Frenchman could never have learned in Hamburg. The detective then made his way to the nearest police station and requested that a muscular constable spend a couple of nights with him inside the Sauber workshop. He was expecting a break-in.

That same night, at 3 a.m., the tinker from the Vendée was arrested and charged with breaking and entering. Other charges followed.

What was going on?

THE ADVENTURE OF THE ATHENIAN BUST

As we have noted elsewhere, Sherlock Holmes was never happier than when in London. The further from the capital he went, the more uncomfortable he became. It was with extreme reluctance, therefore, that he travelled to Athens in the spring of 1903. Watson suggests he undertook the long and laborious journey solely at the request of his brother Mycroft, who was a close friend of a couple urgently needing Holmes's help.

The couple in question were Mr and Mrs Zitomir d'Arche, renowned collectors of artefacts from the ancient world. Backed by the fortune Mrs d'Arche's father had made in South Africa, they had accumulated the finest collection of authentic ancient busts of Greek philosophers in all Europe. Aristotle, Socrates, Pythagoras, and twenty others stood on purpose-made Doric plinths in the panelled gallery of Leighton Abbey, the d'Arche country mansion in Lancashire. Only Plato was missing.

The couple were overjoyed, therefore, when they received a letter from an amateur Albanian archaeologist stating he had uncovered a fine bust of Plato that he was willing to sell. Photographs were sent and the price agreed. Mr d'Arche's secretary, an able young man who five years earlier had won a scholarship to read history at Oxford, went to Albania to confirm the statue's authenticity. After he had assured the d'Arches it was genuine, they decided to combine its purchase with a short holiday. Accordingly, the archaeologist had the artefact crated and shipped to Athens to await their arrival. In mid-April, the d'Arche family and their servants took the *Orient Express* to Constantinople and installed themselves on a steam yacht chartered to convey them to Athens. After a delightful cruise through the Aegean islands, the yacht moored in Piraeus harbour at the end of the month. The bust was carefully ferried aboard and placed on the deck. Mr d'Arche himself opened the crate to inspect his purchase. He declared it to be every bit as fine as he had hoped, and he readily handed over the asking price to the delighted archaeologist.

That evening, the d'Arches held a small drinks reception on board to show off their acquisition. Afterwards, the bust was replaced in its crate. The entire package, measuring approximately three feet by two feet and weighing about

100 pounds, was attached by stout rope to stanchions on either gunwale.

At 5.45 the next morning, the d'Arches were woken by frantic knocking on their cabin door. 'Your statue, sir,' called the captain when asked what the matter was, 'it is not there. In the night, Mr Plato is vanished!'

Holmes, accompanied by a perspiring Watson, reached Athens a fortnight later. The local police, he was told, had shown almost no interest in the theft. Though they never actually said so, Mr d'Arche got the impression they had no wish to assist the sort of plundering of ancient treasures from which Greece itself had suffered so grievously. Regretfully, he concluded, the British detective would have to operate entirely on his own.

Holmes gave a wry smile. 'Not entirely,' he responded, 'for I do have the excellent Doctor Watson to assist me.' The remark turned out to be more prescient than Holmes intended.

It was obvious, he concluded when he had heard the full story, that the theft had been carried out with the help – or at least the knowledge – of someone on board. He was duly presented with a list of those who had slept on the yacht on the night Plato had gone missing:

Mr and Mrs d'Arche
Mr John Harper, Mr d'Arche's secretary
Miss Philippa Bannon, Mrs d'Arche's secretary
The family butler, Thomas Plumber

Two English maids, Ethel Whistler and Lillian Argot
Captain Galanos
Galanos's chief engineer
Two Greek sailors

Holmes interviewed those on the list either personally or, in the case of the engineer and the two deckhands, with the help of an interpreter. Only the secretary, John Harper, was absent: he had already gone back to London to arrange the family's return journey.

During his conversation with Mrs d'Arche, Holmes was told – 'just between you and me, sir' – that she believed Harper and her secretary, 'my lovely, clever, little Philippa', were 'sweet on each other'. She would not be at all surprised if one day soon the pair announced their intention to marry. 'But how they could even consider it on their salaries,' she concluded with a sigh, 'is quite beyond my understanding.'

Holmes nodded and asked why Mrs d'Arche had described Miss Bannon as 'clever'. The lady explained that her secretary always had her 'nose in a book, especially one about history'. She knew as much about ancient Greece as Mr d'Arche, and listening to a conversation between her and Harper was like 'being at a lecture in some college or other'.

Having talked at length to those on his list, Holmes asked to inspect all correspondence, written and telegraphed, that had passed between the ship and shore since they left Constantinople. Though at first the d'Arches objected to handing over their personal letters, they backed down when Holmes said that without their full support he would have little choice but to leave the investigation to someone else.

Holmes spent two hours poring over the pile of papers presented to him. When he had finished, he set aside two of them. Both purported to be about the trains the family should take on their way home. One was a copy of a telegram sent by Philippa Bannon to John Harper. The second was his reply.

Her message ran as follows:

ALL WELL HERE STOP HOLMES LOOKING INTO
THINGS STOP SUGGEST THESE TRAINS PARIS TO
BOULOGNE STOP 15:25 15:71 14:15 04:80 17:08
18:54 18:15 12:63 18:98 16:45 16:50 13:88 18:27 12:98
04:26 18:79 17:06 18:12 16:42 17:09 18:05

Harper's reply read:

THANK YOU FOR MESSAGE STOP ALL READY FOR
FAMILY ARRIVAL STOP BELIEVE THESE TRAIN
TIMES BETTER 17:04 16:43 18:49 18:76 17:75 03:33
17:99 17:00 18:09 13:46 12:17 04:89 12:65 17:98 17:59
16:58 18:07 18:13 02:06 18:63 10:66 14:61 18:00 13:32

Watson was so pleased by his part in what followed that, unusually, he recorded the words of his conversation with Holmes in full.

'Since no clock goes beyond sixty minutes, these numbers are clearly not train times,' the detective began. 'Obviously there's some sort of code here. What do you make of it, Watson?'

'My dear Holmes, you can't possibly expect me to work it out,' came the reply. 'To be perfectly honest, the whole thing looks like a history lesson to me.'

Holmes stared at the telegrams with renewed intensity. 'Good heavens, Watson,' he exclaimed quietly. 'I do believe you're right! Dates! Thank you, old fellow. Let's see if we can work out what events they relate to.'

Holmes and Watson decoded the telegrams with the help of a pile of history books borrowed from Miss Bannon's cabin. Holmes then spoke to Mr d'Arche and went ashore to send a telegram to Scotland Yard. When the collectors and their entourage – minus Miss Bannon – arrived back in England, they found the bust of Plato, undamaged, waiting for them at Leighton Abbey.

What hidden messages had Holmes found that enabled him to solve the case?

THE MYSTERY OF THE VANISHING PHILATELISTS

As readers of the Sherlock Holmes stories are well aware, the respectable public image of late-Victorian Britain was a thin veneer over seething excess and wickedness. No one knew this colourful underworld better than Holmes, and his insight into what motivated some of its more extreme citizens enabled him to solve a case that had baffled Scotland Yard's top people: 'The Mystery of the Vanishing Philatelists'.

In June 1886, the London papers added the name of Jack Durrant, a married clerk from the parish of Newington St Mary, to the city's already long list of missing persons. No further details were given, and such incidents were so common that it attracted minimal attention from the Metropolitan Police. If at the time Sherlock Holmes noticed it, he did not mention the fact to Watson.

In early September of the same year, the police showed a good deal more interest in the unexplained disappearance of one Gregory Billings. The reason for their so doing was that Billings, like Durrant, was also a married clerk from the Newington parish. This unusual coincidence drew the attention of the press and set tongues wagging in the Golden Swan, Cranbury Street, where the two were known to meet and where they had last been seen together. According to their wives, both were keen philatelists, founder members of the Newington Stamp Society, which rented one of the public house's upstairs rooms for its meetings.

Holmes, too, noted the disappearance of the two married philatelists from the same parish. However, apart from making an ironic remark to Watson about the dangers of stamp collecting, he showed no inclination to take the matter further.

Two months passed. Neither Durrant nor Billings reappeared, and a rumour spread among the clientele of the Golden Swan that the pair had run away to Tahiti where, it was said, beautiful young girls threw themselves unreservedly at any foreign man who set foot on the island. John Coleman, the only other regular member of the Newington Stamp Society, mocked such suggestions. Those who made them did not know his friends, he declared. But when asked to give an alternative explanation for the men's disappearance, he frowned and said he didn't have one, but 'something was not right'.

On 5 November, John Coleman learned what that something was. He was not able to pass it on, however, for on that day he too disappeared on his way home to his wife from the Golden Swan. This time the story reached the national press and the Metropolitan Police immediately put two detectives on the case. The following morning, curious to see for himself what was going on, Sherlock Holmes invited Watson to accompany him and took a hansom cab over Southwark Bridge to Newington.

Inspector Lestrade of Scotland Yard was already on the case. He had conducted several interviews with the landlady and regulars of the Golden Swan, but had as yet drawn no firm conclusions. Watson tells us that Holmes met the inspector in the street and offered his services 'as a discreet assistant'. The inspector politely but firmly rejected the offer, saying he could 'manage this one very well on his own'.

Holmes accepted the rebuff with equanimity. Rather than returning to Baker Street, however, he paced the routes the three men would have taken from the Golden Swan to their respective front doors. For the first 400 yards or so, the three paths coincided, passing through a dark, foul-smelling court and rounding a rusty gas-holder before dividing in a small square in front of an oriental-style building in stucco and new brick that proclaimed itself the Temple of Christ Revealed. A poster on a board beside the main doorway informed passers-by that the Temple's current minister was the Highly Reverend Jeremiah St John Woolfstein, 'a preacher of world renown, over from the United States of America to save the souls of this sinful city'.

Watson writes that the detective read the poster carefully and set out to return to the Golden Swan. Ten yards before the entrance to the court, he found his way blocked by a small crowd. In its centre, standing on a wooden box, was the Reverend Jeremiah Woolfstein himself. He was preaching fire and brimstone of the most lurid kind, stating that those who did not heed his words would be punished 'even as it is written in the Book of our Lord God'. Unless Londoners ceased their wicked ways and repented of their sins, he warned, 'the Lord God would surely wipe out their city as he had Sodom and Gomorrah'.

When a woman in the crowd cried out that this was a load of nonsense and the preacher should 'shove off back to America', he pointed a finger at her and shouted, 'Babylon is fallen, is fallen, that great city, because she made all nations drink of the wine of the wrath of her fornication.' In a voice rising to a hysterical scream, he concluded, 'Heed the Book of Revelation, wicked woman! The torment of the ungodly is therein writ.'

Several men and women took exception to this, telling Woolfstein he had no right to insult an honest woman. Finding himself losing the sympathy of the crowd, he changed tactic. He smiled broadly, opened wide his arms and said that all honest Londoners would surely be saved if they followed the straight path of the Lord, a path that led directly to Heaven from the Temple of Christ Revealed.

At this, Watson records, Holmes shook his head, turned on his heel and made his way to the nearest bookshop. Once inside, he informed the proprietor that he was in need of 'some spiritual solace' and wondered if he might browse the religious books section. The man made no objection.

Three days later, on 9 November, the mystery of the vanishing philatelists took a sudden and ghastly turn for the worse. The citizens of the parish of Newington awoke to hear that the bodies of Durrant, Billings and Coleman had been found in Colombo Street, next to Newington Butts. They had been deposited there at some time during the night, propped in a sitting position with their backs against lampposts. Though the first two were in advanced stages of decomposition, it was clear that all three had been horribly mutilated at the time of death.

Shortly after breakfast, a visibly shaken Inspector Lestrade called on Holmes and asked for assistance. He knew stamp collections were valuable, but he had never come across anyone prepared to murder to get hold of one. He had no obvious leads, and 'the public were demanding that the perpetrator of these horrible crimes be swiftly apprehended and brought to justice'.

Holmes agreed to help the desperate officer. He declared with a twinkle in his eye that, though he could offer no guarantees, he had one or two promising lines of enquiry to pursue.

First, he examined the corpses of the missing men. The ribs and sternum of Jack Durrant were broken in several places, suggesting the body had been crushed beneath a heavy weight. In contrast, the desiccated remains of Gregory Billings appeared to bear no unusual marks at all. However, peering closely at the wrists with his magnifying glass, Holmes identified a series of minute punctures. A single glance at the body of John Coleman was sufficient to reveal the cause of his death. His feet and the lower part of his legs had been burned away, and the look of unspeakable anguish frozen on his face told that he had died in great agony.

From the mortuary where the bodies had been taken, Holmes went to a local lending library. Here he consulted the final section of a very large and very black King James Bible, and copied out a few verses, together with their numbers, on to a piece of paper. He then returned to Newington to question the wives of the deceased. It was a painful process involving much weeping and commiseration, but in the end he drew forth the answers he needed. Jack Durrant had disappeared on the night of Wednesday 16 June. Mrs Durrant said he had been attending a meeting of the NSS, the Newington Stamp Society, in the Golden Swan. His stamp collection, which he always kept in a leather bag out of the sight of her and the children, was not in the house. As Mrs Durrant had previously explained to Inspector Lestrade, she assumed her husband's attacker must have stolen it.

Mrs Billings gave similar responses. Her husband had left home on Sunday 5 September to attend a meeting of the NSS in the Golden Swan, a gathering from which he had never returned. His stamp collection, which Mrs Billings had never seen but which her husband always carried in a canvas holdall, was also missing.

Holmes met Watson on his way to interview Mrs Coleman. 'I feel the noose drawing tighter about the criminal's neck,' he confided eagerly. 'I require but two more pieces of evidence, and I will then be able to hand the matter over to Lestrade to make the arrests.'

Mrs Coleman, whose husband had gone missing just

three days previously and who had learned of his horrible death only that morning, was too distressed to discuss her beloved John's movements with anyone. Fortunately for Holmes, her elder sister, Mrs Winnifred Pollard, who lived just three doors further down the street, was more than willing to talk. Yes, she knew all about her brother-in-law's membership of the NSS and his attendance at its meetings in the upper room of the Golden Swan. And, no, as far as she was aware, her sister showed no interest in his stamp collection. Mrs Coleman had never actually seen it, though she knew her husband always took it to meetings in a calfskin briefcase.

Holmes thanked Mrs Pollard for her help and walked briskly to the Golden Swan. The landlady, a God-fearing

Anglican who refused to serve alcohol on Sundays or saints' days, was happy to repeat to Holmes all she had already told Inspector Lestrade. She had let the Newington Stamp Society hire her upper room for a monthly fee of two shillings. The society's three members had kept themselves to themselves and never caused her any trouble.

Had she ever seen their stamp collections?

No, she had not. The men went to great lengths to keep their books hidden. Once, when she interrupted one of their meetings to ask whether she could bring them a cup of tea, Coleman had gone so far as to throw his jacket over the table to hide what lay there.

This did not strike her as odd?

'A bit, perhaps,' the woman confessed. 'But I didn't mind because they were such kind gentlemen. In fact,' she went on, 'several months ago they were good enough to come to my aid.'

Holmes asked her to explain. At the beginning of June, she said, shortly after his arrival in England, the Reverend Woolfstein had begun his mission to London by preaching outside the Golden Swan. The public house, he declared, was a den of iniquity, a cesspool of drunkards and harlots presided over by a shameless servant of the spawn of Rome.

The landlady went outside to protest, asking him to move away. His refusal, accompanied by a stream of biblical invective, was overheard by the three members of the NSS as they arrived for one of their meetings. They immediately came to their hostess's rescue. They mocked the preacher by quoting bits of the Bible at him. Their knowledge of Holy Scripture surprised her, for she had never seen any of them in church. After a fiery exchange of biblical insults, Woolfstein climbed down from his box and stalked away. The landlady saw Billings try to thrust a leaflet into his hand. The preacher glanced at it, then scowled at his three persecutors before disappearing in the direction of his Temple. As the landlady went back inside, she noticed her gallant rescuers handing out further leaflets to the crowd.

'Did she see what these were?' Holmes asked.

'Not really,' she replied. She assumed they were invitations to join the Stamp Society because they had NSS in large letters at the top of them.

On hearing this, Holmes thanked the woman for her clear and helpful responses. Half an hour later, having called in at the local library again to check the names of organizations with the acronym NSS, he caught up with Lestrade and suggested he arrest the Reverend Woolfstein and his close followers for murder, and then carry out a very careful search of the Temple of Christ Revealed.

Three months later, Reverend Woolfstein and three of his congregation were hanged for the abduction and murder of Jack Durrant, Gregory Billings and John Coleman.

How had Holmes deduced the guilt of the preacher and his accomplices?

A CASE OF BANANAS

Most of the cases on which Holmes worked came directly to him, often by a personal visit, a letter or a telegram. 'A Case of Bananas' was an exception. Holmes brought his involvement in this singular case upon himself through his habit of spending time every morning carefully reading the day's papers.

On one such occasion, his attention was drawn to a short report in the *Daily Chronicle* of Thursday 29 August 1895. The item read:

Death by Misadventure

Ruling on the unfortunate demise of Dr Robert Matteson on 15 August last, the coroner, Mr William Dennis, declared a verdict of 'Death by Misadventure'. The ruling comes as no surprise to us. Readers may well remember that Dr Matteson, an enthusiast for what he keenly advocated to be a healthy diet, received regular shipments of exotic fruits from the colonies. On the day of his death he took possession of a case of several bunches of bananas from Jamaica. Two young, venomous spiders had remained undetected within the fruit when it was picked, shipped across the Atlantic and unloaded at Tilbury. It was Dr Matteson's extreme misfortune, as he plucked a single banana from one of the bunches, for his hand to come into contact with both these deadly creatures at the same time. Fully grown men have been known to survive the bite of a single Banana Spider, but the venom of two is surely fatal. So it proved with Dr Matteson, who died within the hour.

While Watson found the story sad but unremarkable, it set Holmes off on a trail that led to Dr Matteson's wife, Dorothy, and her lover, George Gilbertson, being found guilty of murder and hanged.

When the case was over, Watson, once again astounded by his friend's powers of detection, asked what made him suspect foul play in the first place.

We are told that at this point Holmes gave a wry smile and lit his pipe. 'Elementary, my dear Watson,' he is reported to have said, using his now world-famous catchphrase. 'My suspicions were aroused the moment I read how the unfortunate Mr Matteson died ...'

Murder in Room 327

On Friday 14 March 1879, the young Sherlock Holmes was leaving Scotland Yard after a meeting with Lestrade when he was buttonholed by another detective, the elderly Douglas Grimes.

Grimes had been in the force for longer than anyone could remember, and he teased Holmes in a good-natured way about his youth and lack of experience. 'You could learn a lot from me, young man,' he boasted. 'There's not a man alive as knows the criminal world of the capital better than I do. Why, Holmes, I often has to do no more than look at a crime to solve it.

'Take the one I'm presently dealing with … I've already got a pretty good idea of what happened. Why don't you come along with me and see how it's done?'

Holmes later told Watson that he accepted Grimes's invitation in order to learn how *not* to investigate a crime.

As they travelled towards the crime scene, the portly Grimes related what he knew of the case. That morning,

Albert Higginbottom, a thirty-year-old married arms manufacturer from Sheffield, had been found dead in Room 327 of the Royal Staffordshire Hotel behind Soho Square. He had been stabbed through the throat with a bayonet manufactured by his own company. The blow had been sufficiently powerful to sever his carotid artery and leave the tip of the weapon wedged between two vertebrae in his neck.

The doctor who attended the scene declared that Mr Higginbottom had died instantaneously. He also noted deep scratches on the victim's right cheek and left hand; he estimated these wounds had been inflicted between thirty-six and seventy-two hours previously, a good deal earlier than the fatal stabbing. Glancing beneath the dead man's nightshirt, the doctor also observed that he was infected with syphilis.

There were no signs that anything had been taken from the room, which ruled out the motive of theft.

A crumpled photograph from Higginbottom's wallet showed him in a dark suit standing next to a pretty lady in a wedding dress and a smartly dressed young man. The bride and the younger man, hand in hand, were so similar in stature and appearance – straight fair hair and innocent, almost child-like faces – that they had to be twins. On the back of the picture, '21 July 1878' was written in red pencil.

The other item of interest in the wallet was a bill from Dr James Gumpert of 25 Ribble Mansions, Sheffield, dated 8 March, 'for the setting of a fractured forearm'. The doctor examining Higginbottom's corpse said neither of the deceased's forearms had ever been set.

Higginbottom's valise contained only clothing. In his briefcase were a catalogue of products manufactured by Higginbottom & Co., and a letter from a Mr Mustafa Tekin about meeting in the Midland Grand Hotel on Wednesday 12 March to discuss the purchase of 500,000 rounds of bullets.

Holmes and Grimes arrived at the hotel to find that the body had been removed, but not the deceased's personal effects. While Grimes went to speak to the porter who had been on duty that night, Holmes examined the bayonet and catalogue.

Using a lens, he could make out the inscription 'Hig no. 11,004 69' on the blade of the weapon. Finding 'bayonets' in the catalogue, he noted that a large batch of these weapons – numbers 11,006–15,000 – were marked as 'all sold'. A footnote explained that numbers 11,000–11,005 were samples ('not for sale'), and bayonet production had been discontinued in 1876.

Holmes came downstairs to find Grimes in an office behind the reception desk, interviewing a rather nervous porter. The man knew the late Mr Higginbottom 'rather well' as the gentleman had stayed at the Royal Staffordshire several times during the past year. Three nights was his customary length of stay, and each time – including the recent one – a young lady had visited him in his room. Always veiled and wearing a dark, ankle-length coat, she generally arrived around 11 o'clock and departed three to four hours later. On each occasion, apart from the last, she slipped a half-crown into his hand as she left.

Grimes mopped his brow and asked about the previous night's visit. The porter said the lady had arrived later than usual, just before midnight, and stayed only fifteen minutes.

Had he spoken to her? No, she had entered quietly while he was reading the *Evening Standard*, and he noticed her only as she was disappearing up the stairs. She left in a great hurry, saying not a word and forgetting her customary tip.

Grimes mopped his brow again. Did the porter have the lady's address? When the man hesitated, Grimes told him not to be foolish and made unsubtle threats about the penalties for pimping. At this, the porter said the hotel was eager to provide whatever its guests required and, yes, he did know the address of a lady who offered a laundry service. She might be the person whom the gentlemen were looking for.

As Holmes and Grimes were leaving the hotel, a constable appeared with a telegram. Addressed to Grimes, it was Mrs Higginbottom's reply to his request that she come to London at her earliest convenience to help the police in a matter concerning her husband.

'We need someone to formally identify the body,' Grimes explained. 'Always remember that when you're on a case, Holmes.'

Mrs Higginbottom's telegram read as follows:

APOLOGIES UNABLE TO TRAVEL STOP BADLY INJURED IN CAB ACCIDENT STOP BROTHER TOM WILL TAKE MY PLACE STOP EXPECT HIM HERE SOON STOP WILL ARRIVE ST PANCRAS TONIGHT STOP AGNES HIGGINBOTTOM

Grimes declared that a brother-in-law would serve as well as a wife, and invited Holmes to accompany him in the arrest of the 'laundry woman'. Holmes looked somewhat startled at this and said that, if Grimes would excuse him, he had some business of his own to attend to.

After sending two telegrams, one to Dr Gumpert and another to the central police station, Sheffield, Holmes went to the public conveniences at St Pancras station. He started with the male facilities and engaged the attendant in a long conversation about the vagaries of his occupation. The detective said he bet the fellow encountered all kinds of bizarre goings on.

'Oh yes, sir,' came the gleeful reply. 'Only yesterday this girly-looking man comes in with a large valise, goes into a cubicle, and comes out dressed as a woman!'

Having learned that the transformation took place at about 11 p.m., that the man was fair-haired, short in stature, and departed wearing a veil and a long dark coat, Holmes thanked the attendant for providing him with 'such a fascinating insight into human nature' and moved over to the Ladies.

Here the task was more difficult. The woman who had been on duty since 10 p.m. on Thursday night had now gone home, and her replacement was suspicious of any man loitering near her conveniences and attempting to draw her into conversation. After resisting Holmes's enquiries for five minutes, she said they'd had enough trouble recently – 'what with some homosexual in women's clothes sneaking in this morning while poor Marj's back was turned' – and if Holmes did not 'shove off sharpish' she'd call the police.

Holmes apologized for distressing her, thanked her for her help, and promptly left. On his way to Scotland

Yard, he called in at Baker Street to collect the replies to his telegrams. That from the Sheffield Constabulary read simply: NOTHING REPORTED OR ON RECORD.

Dr Gumpert was even less forthcoming: CANNOT REVEAL DETAILS OF CASES TO STRANGERS STOP ESPECIALLY THOSE OF A LADY STOP APOLOGIES

Holmes found Grimes waiting for him at the Yard, beaming like an oversized cherub. 'Told you it was plain as a pikestaff, didn't I, Holmes? Take a leaf out of old Grimes's book: there's nearly always a wicked woman behind every crime. In our case it's Maggie Jones.'

He explained that when arrested, Miss Jones confessed to

having visited Albert Higginbottom several times when he was in London, but swore she had not gone to Room 327 last night because a baby-faced gentleman with a northern accent had called on her, paid her handsomely, and said his friend Mr Higginbottom did not require her services that evening.

Could anyone corroborate her story? Grimes had asked. Did she have an alibi? No, of course not. She had obviously argued furiously with Higginbottom, the detective explained, probably about money, and stabbed him with one of his own bayonets when he refused to pay what she thought she was worth. She wasn't going to tip the porter on a night she hadn't been paid, was she? Her tale about money from a mysterious gentleman 'was typical of the sort of unlikely story them types come up with'.

'That may often be true,' observed Holmes, 'but in this instance I believe the young lady was telling the truth. You have arrested the wrong person, Grimes!'

What evidence did Holmes have for this remark, and who did he believe had murdered the Sheffield arms manufacturer?

THE FRAUDSTER'S FINGER

Umbrigg Vaultson, noted Watson, had many enemies. According to a City friend of the doctor's, the self-made millionaire had made his fortune by persuading hundreds of ordinary citizens to invest their lifetime's savings in a scheme optimistically entitled 'Everyman's Wealth Generator'. Quite how the arrangement would create wealth for anyone but its originator was never clear, and when the scheme collapsed in 1889, leaving many of its patrons destitute, wise heads in Threadneedle Street tutted and said they had seen it coming from the beginning.

Vaultson, unaffected by the collapse, set himself up in two ostentatious households, one at 14 Berkeley Square, London, and the other at Fortune Towers, a neo-Gothic mansion near the Hertfordshire town of Berkhamsted. For a while it appeared that he had got away with his gigantic swindle unscathed. Then, at 5.30 p.m. on 23 February 1879, as he was being driven up the long approach to his country seat, he was kidnapped.

The attack was carefully planned. Rounding a bend in the tree-lined drive, Vaultson's coach was stopped by three masked men on horseback. One stood guard while the other two, brandishing pistols, pulled open the coach door, grabbed Vaultson and dragged him outside.

At that moment, a cart bearing the millionaire's baggage rumbled up the drive behind them. This was clearly a surprise to the kidnappers – Vaultson's effects were usually sent on ahead – and they panicked.

While the two taller assailants forced their victim at gunpoint to lie across the saddle of a waiting horse and knocked him unconscious with a vicious blow to the head,

the third attacker pulled two papers from his jacket pocket and threw them on to the seat of the carriage. He then cursed and made to retrieve one of the documents. Before he could do so, he was urgently called away by the others, and the three villains galloped off into the darkness with the unconscious body of Umbrigg Vaultson.

As soon as they were alone, the postilion and the manservant who had been riding beside him examined the papers left inside the coach. The first was a straightforward ransom note, spelled out in letters cut from the *Daily Telegraph* and glued to a sheet of notepaper. It demanded £50,000 in cash within a week. If the police were informed or the money not paid, the captive would be killed.

The second paper contained two rows of random letters above a drawing of a 'bulger' golf club:

TDEPOARFMURIITGGVFH
EETUTFERIIESNVND

Vaultson's wife and her two sons ignored the second paper as some sort of draft version of the ransom note. They ignored the ransom itself, too, until, a week after the hijack, an anonymous parcel was delivered to Fortune Towers.

Inside was one of the millionaire's fingers, sawn off below the knuckle, and a cut-and-paste note saying that more body parts would follow until the ransom was paid.

The next day, Mrs Vaultson and her elder son called on Sherlock Holmes to ask for his assistance. Though the detective had little liking for the crooked millionaire, he liked crime even less and – after agreeing an appropriate fee for his services – undertook to investigate the case in strictest confidence.

He immediately focused on the lines of random letters on the second paper found in the coach. Having considered them for a while, he went to work with pen, paper, scissors – and a golf club. When he had finished, he wired Mrs Vaultson enquiring whether she had a man named Douglas on her staff. The reply came back almost immediately: yes, six months ago they had taken on Douglas Telford as a tutor for their youngest child.

'Which means, my dear Watson,' said Holmes with a wry smile, 'that we are well on the way to concluding this whole unsavoury business.'

What had Holmes discovered?

THE MYSTERY OF THE
MISSING MASTERPIECES

For several years, Watson believed Holmes knew nothing of art. His view changed after *The Hound of the Baskervilles* case, in which the detective correctly identified the work of distinguished painters. The doctor was only mildly surprised, therefore, when a court official contacted Holmes to ask for help in recovering four seventeenth-century masterpieces stolen from the royal collection housed in Windsor Castle. They were estimated to be worth a considerable six-figure sum.

At the request of the Prince of Wales, the theft had been kept quiet. Nevertheless, customs officers in every port were alerted and told to keep a sharp lookout. Specifically, they were instructed to search the luggage and effects of well-known art collectors leaving the country.

After Holmes had agreed to take on the case, he was provided with further details. The stolen works, all invaluable and in elaborate gilt frames, were representations of female nudes. The smallest was 3 feet 6 inches × 2 feet 3½ inches (1.07 metres × 0.45 metres), and the largest 8 feet × 5 feet 6 inches (2.44 metres × 1.67 metres). The other two were both the same size, 4 feet 7½ inches × 3 feet 9 inches (1.41 metres × 1.14 metres).

The robbery had been executed at night with meticulous precision by skilled art thieves who had bribed a castle guard. Such criminals, Holmes knew, invariably operated with a purchaser in mind. After the official had left Baker Street, Holmes mined his newspaper cuttings to produce a shortlist of collectors of Rembrandts, Van Dycks and other seventeenth-century masters.

Holmes reckoned it extremely likely the pictures had been stolen to order by someone on his list. Furthermore, as whoever had taken them would surely wish to display them rather than keep them locked in a cellar, UK residents could be discounted. Holmes showed the remaining names to a contact who worked at the National Gallery. Without revealing his motive, he asked which of the people on the list were known to acquire works in Britain and ship them abroad. The response enabled him to cut his list to ten.

The next step was to ask Scotland Yard about the probity of those names. He was told that seven had no criminal records, yet three of them had either fallen foul of the law in the past or were under serious suspicion. One of these three, the Italian Duke of Capraia, had been murdered the previous year, so this left just two suspects: Hildereena Granwerther of New Jersey and Count Lekszi Végh of Budapest.

Holmes knew it was perfectly possible both were innocent, but having little else to go on, he persevered with his line of enquiry and soon had substantial files on the American and the Hungarian. And the more he learned, the surer he felt one of them was behind the theft.

Mrs Granwerther's money had come from her deceased husband, a highly successful manufacturer of rivets. After his passing, she had gone into real estate and increased her fortune ten-fold through a series of deals that, allegedly, involved extortion and even murder. When the eastern seaboard of the United States became too hot for her, she had moved to Paris and concentrated for a while on building up her collection of fine art and antique furniture.

After two years, seeking another challenge, Mrs Granwerther bought a second home, in London, and moved into the English real estate business, again with remarkable success. However, rumours were already circulating that, as in the United States, her methods were less than scrupulous. Critics said the way she was adding to her priceless collection of paintings and furniture back in Paris was equally dubious, and all respectable galleries and auction houses now refused to work with her. Nevertheless, her thirst for new acquisitions remained unquenched.

Count Lekszi Végh was a much more straightforward

character. He made no effort to hide the fact that he held the law, at home and in Britain, in utter contempt. He had inherited a vast estate back home in Hungary, at the centre of which was a palace that he boasted he would make the 'art capital of the world'. To bring this about he used the family fortune augmented by money made by trading in armaments and, it was said, slaves, to acquire works of art, furniture and tapestries wherever he could find them. The Italian police were sure that the recent disappearance from the Vatican of works by Raphael, Tintoretto and Titian was Végh's work. Like Mrs Granwerther, the count was *persona non grata* at all of London's major galleries and auction houses.

Holmes knew, as did his suspects, that on leaving the country their possessions would be thoroughly searched. If one of them had the stolen paintings, he asked himself, how would they try to get them out of the country? The answer would be to conceal them somewhere no customs officer would think of looking, hidden in something that did not even belong to one of the suspects or had been in their possession for only a very short time.

Gibbins and Dang, a small auction house in the London parish of Whitechapel, was one of the few that still agreed to work with Mrs Granwerther and Count Végh. Holmes gathered this while putting together his files on the suspects, and when he learned that G & D (as they were popularly known) were holding a sale of eighteenth-century French furniture in two weeks' time, he told Watson he might need to attend. First, however, he had to carry out one more investigation.

Sporting a neat moustache and dressed in the brown linen coat of a master furniture maker, Holmes called at the London residence of his two suspects. Had they any items of antique furniture in need of repair? In both cases he drew a blank.

Mrs Granwerther's housekeeper assured him the furniture in her care was in perfect condition. The manager of the count's household, a red-faced former soldier with one arm, told Holmes in broken English that three weeks previously all pieces needing repair had been sent to a private workshop. No, he would not answer any more rude questions, and unless Mr Makepiece (as Holmes had styled himself) left the premises immediately, he would call the police.

That evening at supper, the detective assured Watson that his visits had been 'most enlightening' and he would be attending the Gibbins and Dang auction.

On the morning of the sale, Holmes emerged from his dressing room as M. Vincent de Béarn, a flamboyant Parisian art dealer. After testing his accent on Mrs Hudson, who understood not a word he said, he took a cab to the saleroom.

He arrived in good time, introduced himself to the auctioneer and his staff, and proceeded to inspect the items on offer. He showed special interest in a Louis XIV table with elaborately carved legs, two high-backed chairs from the reign of Louis XV, and a Louis XVI *chaise longue*. After examining each piece with his magnifying glass, Holmes carefully lifted the chairs off the ground, ostensibly to examine their feet. Finally, he underlined the reserve prices in his catalogue and took his seat in the hall.

Fifteen lots came under the hammer before M. de Béarn showed much interest in the proceedings. By this time, Mrs

Granwerther and the count had each acquired three small pieces. None of the fifteen lots had sold for more than a few pounds above its reserve.

Lot no. 16 was the pair of Louis XV chairs. The American and the Hungarian bid against each other for a while, driving the price to a respectable £175. At this point, Mrs Granwerther dropped out. The count allowed himself a satisfied smile as his bid was called for the second time.

Before the hammer came down, and to the astonishment of everyone in the room, M. de Béarn entered with an offer of £180. The count frowned and went to £185. The Parisian sighed and offered £200. By now, the chairs were considerably above their reserve.

To the interest and amusement of the rest of the room, the battle between the dapper Frenchman and the dour Hungarian continued for another seven minutes. In the end, the Hungarian won, but not until the unexceptional pieces had reached a record £690.

At this point, M. de Béarn rose, nodded to the auctioneer, and left the room. On the way out, he was heard to whisper politely to his rival, 'I am *désolé*, Monsieur le Comte. Congratulations on your purchase – *mais je suis* certain that they are valuable a lot more than the money you are paying, *n'est pas?*'

The count gave the man a suspicious look and turned his attention back to the auction. There were other pieces he wished to purchase.

The next morning, following a police raid on the premises of Gibbins and Dang, where the items sold at the previous day's auction were still held, Count Lekszi Végh was arrested and charged with receiving stolen goods – four seventeenth-century masterpieces taken from the royal collection a month earlier.

The police had acted on a tip-off from Sherlock Holmes. What evidence of the count's culpability had he presented them with?

The Case of the Beaded Egg

Watson's notes reveal that on several occasions Sherlock Holmes was brought in to clear things up after blunders by the regular police. One such instance arose from the violent yet avoidable death of the well-known London criminal Charles Stannard-Smith, aka 'Culture Charlie'.

Smith was acknowledged as one of the most intelligent – and eccentric – criminals of his generation. The suave and sophisticated Old Etonian made money from clever swindles, most connected to the operations of his 'Spinner' gambling clubs. The police knew he broke the law, the press knew he broke the law, the politicians and the civil service knew he broke the law, yet he managed to evade arrest for over forty years. Indeed, he was often seen in the highest society, regularly attending the opera, in which he was an acknowledged expert, at Covent Garden.

Unlike most who made their fortune through illegal activities, Smith invested his ill-gotten gains in profitable businesses. He owned four Parisian-style cafés – the Ace, the King, the Queen and the Knave – and four smart hotels named after the suits in a pack of cards. Whether the Hearts Hotel in Soho Square was actually a brothel was never quite clear. Nor did Smith attempt to clarify the matter, explaining that a little bit of mystery was good for business.

It was not the Hearts that finally brought about Smith's demise, but the Diamonds, his flagship hotel in Hanover Square. All Smith's cafés and hotels were decorated with a lavish jumble of what can loosely be described as 'works of art'. These ranged from straightforward paintings to carved elephant tusks, mechanical toys, and mannequins dressed (some scandalously undressed) in exotic costumes from various corners of the globe. The central feature of the Diamonds Hotel was a large glass case at the head of the main stairway bearing the label 'Reserved for the World's Most Beautiful Diamond'.

For five years, the case remained empty while Smith, in his own words, 'searched for a jewel sufficiently elegant to grace my fine hotel'. He let the criminal underworld know that he would be happy to pay handsomely for a stone of suitable brilliance, whatever its provenance. The police blamed the offer for a sharp rise in the number of thefts, actual and attempted, from high-class jewellers throughout the capital.

In the most daring of these robberies, the thieves got away

with a four-carat Radiant diamond worth many thousands of pounds. When arrested a week later, the thieves confessed to the crime and said they had passed the diamond on to 'a gentleman who worked for Culture Charlie'.

Unwisely, the job of questioning Smith about the stolen jewel was given to a young detective of abrupt manner and considerable physical strength. The conversation between the muscular policeman and the sleek, overweight criminal-businessman became heated. Frustrated by Smith's condescending attitude and obvious scorn for his ignorance of both the law and English grammar, the detective sprang to his feet and grabbed his tormentor by the throat. The action

proved fatal – Smith suffered a massive heart attack and never recovered consciousness.

The officer was dismissed from the force. More significantly, the whereabouts of the diamond remained a mystery.

At this point, Scotland Yard asked Sherlock Holmes for help. The great detective, who had made a private study of Smith's intriguing personality and jocular habits, was sure he would have left a clue as to the diamond's whereabouts. He began his search in Smith's vast and cluttered bachelor bedchamber in a suite on the fifth floor of the Ace Café. Magnifying glass in hand, he scrutinized every *objet d'art* and gaudy knick-knack. He was intrigued by a gold and ivory inlaid musical box. Finding a key beneath the pillows on Smith's luxurious bed, he opened the lid and allowed the strangely formless music to play. He repeated the action, this time using his knowledge of music to jot down the notes:

After listening to the music a third time and amending what he had written, Holmes walked over to a silver birdcage containing a stuffed macaw that hung beside the wash basin. Beneath the cage was a large, Chinese-style porcelain egg somewhat faded by age. It was exquisitely decorated with a dozen beaded mouldings representing the life cycle of the bee. The last of these showed a dead bee, on its back with its legs in the air.

Holmes carefully pressed the body of the final bee, and the top of the egg sprang open to reveal the missing diamond nestling in a bed of cotton wool.

How on earth had he worked out what to do?

THE MYSTERY OF THE FALLEN SERGEANT

Canterton Cathedral, though the leading church of the Anglican Communion, rarely made the headlines. It was with some surprise, therefore, that on Tuesday 20 April 1886, Watson found the building featuring prominently in all the daily papers. The reason was the discovery, early the previous day, of a dead body on the stone floor of the cathedral's transept.

Watson was even more surprised when, on the Friday of the same week, his friend Sherlock Holmes received a visit from Detective Frank Blean of the Kent Constabulary. 'The Mystery of the Fallen Sergeant', as the press were calling it, had put him under unaccustomed pressure, and he was not sure his nerves could take it much longer. Put very simply, while he regarded the case as anything but clear-cut, his superiors and 'all the city bigwigs' were urging him to declare it to be one of suicide.

Holmes felt an instinctive liking for the honest, straightforward Blean, who was obviously out of his depth, and agreed to help him. To do so openly would incur the wrath of the 'bigwigs', and land Blean in even greater trouble. He would get round the problem, he told Watson, by visiting the ancient city of St Egfrith, Plankton and Henley, in disguise. Impressive-looking credentials were swiftly created, and on Saturday morning William Hoffenbach III, European correspondent of the *New England Telegraph*, caught the 10.10 from Victoria to Canterton West.

Blean's account, together with reports in the press, had furnished Holmes with a good deal of information about the case.

At 7.30 a.m. on Monday 19 April, the cathedral verger, Clarence Flipp, had discovered the body of Sergeant Robert Melrose of the Rifle Brigade lying dead on the south side of the cathedral transept. His pockets were empty, as was the money belt he wore beneath his army uniform. Holmes had pressed Blean on this point. Was he certain it was a money belt?

Absolutely certain, the detective replied.

And it was completely empty?

Completely.

Holmes paused for a moment before asking his visitor to continue. The body's broken bones and final posture left Blean in no doubt that Melrose had fallen from the clerestory above. Perhaps surprisingly, he had not died immediately. Using the fingers of his right hand, smeared with blood seeping from his fractured skull, the dying man had written the word MASS on the stone flags beside him. A silver chalice of great antiquity and value lay a short distance away. Clearly damaged by falling from a great height, it was identified as belonging to the cathedral's collection of plate. Over the past month, a fifteenth-century gold cross and a second silver chalice, similar to that found beside Melrose's body, had also gone missing.

Once again Holmes checked the details of the case.

Blean was sure the chalice had fallen from the clerestory?

As sure as he could be without having been there to witness it. There was even a small chip in the flagstone where it had landed.

And there was nothing else but the word 'MASS' written in blood?

There was some sort of squiggle after the final S. Blean assumed it was the dying man's attempt to conclude his message with a full stop.

Holmes nodded but made no comment.

By the evening of the same day, the city's inns and taverns were buzzing with stories about the 'Fallen Sergeant'. Everyone appeared to know Melrose was a 'ladies' man'. He was said to have fathered several illegitimate children in Britain and overseas, and to have a wife and family in his native Scotland as well as the one he lived with in Canterton, where his regiment was based. It was obvious, ran the gossip, that as he could not maintain his dependants on a sergeant's pay, he had taken to thieving.

The cathedral, with its priceless collection of antique treasure, was a ready target. Having successfully lifted the cross and the chalice, the sergeant had met his comeuppance when attempting to steal a second chalice. Further proof of the validity of this version of events came from Father Dominic, the priest in charge of Canterton's Roman Catholic church. Robert Melrose was a Catholic, making his presence in the Anglican cathedral even more suspicious. Father Dominic suggested Melrose's scrawling of MASS as he lay dying had been a confession of guilt and a plea for mercy from the Almighty.

Holmes agreed with Blean that although the popular version of events was superficially plausible, it left several important facts unexplained. How had Melrose got into the cathedral? Why was he wearing a money belt? And what on earth was he doing up in the clerestory when the plate was kept in the treasury beside the crypt? In the opinion of the press, these questions would never be answered because the only person who could do so was dead.

The European correspondent of the *New England Telegraph* thought otherwise.

Having taken a room at the Bardolph Hotel near the city's West Gate, Holmes made his way to the cathedral precincts and asked to speak to the verger. Clarence Flipp duly appeared. His initial reluctance to talk to a newspaper correspondent evaporated when Hoffenbach casually mentioned that he planned to run his piece on the Fallen Sergeant case under the title 'Why did the verger allow a thief to enter his cathedral?'

Flipp, whom Holmes considered far too virtuous to have been party to Melrose's supposed robberies, revealed several interesting pieces of information. The body had certainly not been there when he locked up after evensong on Sunday evening, and when he and the police searched the building, they found no sign of a break-in. The only people with keys to the cathedral were himself, the dean, and two of the canons. One of the latter was the eighty-nine-year-old Canon Collins, who nowadays rarely left his rooms. The other, Canon Adams, had recently married and was away in Devon on honeymoon.

And the dean? enquired Hoffenbach, licking the tip of his pencil with professional expertise. What could Mr Flipp tell him about Dean Garfield-Wolkes?

The Very Reverend Simon Arbuthnot Garfield-Wolkes, the verger said, was a truly remarkable man. From a

distinguished Herefordshire family, he had joined the Royal
Welsh Fusiliers at the age of twenty and served with distinction
on several campaigns. The last of these, the Ashanti War of
1873–4, had filled him with such a strong dislike of all things
military that he had resigned his commission and entered
the church. From that moment forwards, he had declared,
he would devote himself to the ways of peace, not war.

About the precincts, Garfield-Wolkes cut quite a figure.
His tall and powerful frame, invariably topped by a broad-
brimmed black hat, was unmistakable. And when he spoke,
the ancient stonework echoed to the sound of his stentorian
voice. He modelled it, he said, on that of his regimental
sergeant-major.

There was, however, another side to the man's character.
On several occasions, the verger had found him alone in
the cathedral, on his knees, praying with burning intensity.
Once, when Flipp had inadvertently disturbed him, the ex-
soldier, who was known to have a quick temper, had flown
into a rage. He quickly calmed down and apologized, saying
he was always a bit on edge when asking God to forgive the
many and heinous sins of his campaigning days.

Holmes saw for himself the formidable dean in action
when he attended matins the following morning and heard
him preach. The sermon was undoubtedly impressive, a
fine example of what was coming to be known as 'muscular
Christianity'. It did not refer directly to the death of Sergeant
Melrose, but its text from the Book of Numbers – 'Be sure

your sin will find you out' – left few doubting the dean's meaning. He closed his address by pointing theatrically to the faint bloodstains still visible on the transept floor.

Holmes joined other members of the congregation invited to take tea in the deanery drawing room that afternoon. He had little opportunity to speak to the dean himself, but he did fall into conversation with his wife, the Honourable Susan Garfield-Wolkes. She was surprisingly outspoken, probably because she believed she was addressing an American – someone she believed to be likeminded – and confessed to finding her social obligations 'frightfully tedious'.

'And to make matters worse, Mr Offenbach,' she went on, 'I'm expected to pay for it all!'

The European correspondent of the *New England Telegraph* ignored the mispronunciation of his name and asked her what she meant.

'Oh, he doesn't like to admit it, but Simon doesn't have a bean of his own. He's always coming to me for money for some hare-brained scheme or other.'

Holmes also learned that, in the morning, the dean was going to Lambeth Palace, London, to discuss the Melrose affair with the archbishop. As soon as the Canterton telegraph office opened, Holmes sent Watson a telegram asking him to position himself on Victoria station between 10 a.m. and noon, and let him know if a tall gentleman wearing clerical garb and a broad black hat alighted from one of the Canterton trains.

Watson did as Holmes requested, and reported that he had seen no such figure. A further telegram followed, asking the doctor to enquire whether a man fitting the same description had been seen at London Bridge station that morning. At 4.25 p.m., Watson telegraphed to say that, yes, a ticket inspector at London Bridge did remember seeing a tall vicar in a black hat.

Holmes spent Tuesday in the local library. He read reports of the Third Ashanti War in *The Times* and the *Daily Telegraph*, then wrote a short piece for the *New England Telegraph* entitled 'The Mystery of the Fallen Sergeant'. It began:

When a man is found dead on the floor of an English cathedral, the last person one suspects of bringing about the poor fellow's demise is the dean of that cathedral. Sadly, however, that is precisely what happened in Canterton last week.

Holmes checked through the article, placed it in an envelope addressed to the Very Reverend Simon Garfield-Wolkes, and posted it through the door of the deanery.

When Clarence Flipp opened the cathedral the next morning, he was devastated to find the body of the dean lying on the stone flags of the transept floor. He had fallen from the clerestory and died immediately. Beside him lay the draft of an article written for the *New England Telegraph*.

What did it say?

THE MYSTERY OF THE
THREE TIPSY CLERKS

Watson tells us that several victims of crime approached Sherlock Holmes because they were frightened of going to the police. The doctor's notes relating to one such case appear under the heading 'The Mystery of the Three Tipsy Clerks' – a surprisingly light-hearted title for a story of vicious and premeditated murder.

Early one morning, the terrified Elijah Petrel, a twenty-five-year-old solicitor's clerk, hurried up the steps of 221B Baker Street and hammered frantically on the famous detective's door. 'Please, sir,' he begged, 'let me in and save me from that murdering Indian man.'

Holmes did not normally accept cases presented in such a crude manner, but he was intrigued, and agreed to hear Petrel's story.

It had begun when Petrel and two clerks from the same office, Peter Dimble and Archie Falk, took advantage of a free afternoon to enjoy a long and tipsy luncheon at the Iron Duke tavern, near Euston station. Ambling down the street after the meal, the three bachelors noticed in a pawnbroker's window a ruby and diamond ring of exceptional brilliance. All three coveted the jewel as a betrothal gift for a future fiancée. Unfortunately, not one of them could meet the £150 price tag.

Petrel, Dimble and Falk had a lengthy discussion on a park bench and came to an agreement: they would each contribute £50, a sum they could just afford, and purchase the ring jointly. It would then be safely locked away. The first one to save the £100 needed to buy out the other two would become the ring's sole owner.

The three men duly gathered together all their savings, purchased the ring, and handed it to their employer for safekeeping in the firm's vault.

A week later, the three clerks were having a quick pint in the Iron Duke after work when they were approached by an enormous, bearded Indian in traditional costume. The imposing stranger introduced himself as Amir Asaduddin Khan. He hoped the 'three esteemed gentlemen' would forgive this unannounced interruption, but he believed a local pawnbroker had recently sold them a ring. 'I implore you in the name of the Prophet,' he pleaded, fixing them with his large, flashing eyes, 'to sell me that ring.'

The clerks were taken aback and a little frightened. They would think the matter over, they said, and if Mr Khan came back tomorrow evening, they would give him their answer.

After the giant had gone, the friends realized their ring was probably worth a great deal more than they had paid for it. Consequently, they would not sell. When Khan received this answer, he repeated his request, this time with even greater passion. The answer was still no.

The following morning, Archie Falk did not turn up for work. When after a day or two he had not yet appeared, enquiries were made. They proved fruitless. Archie Falk had disappeared.

Elijah Petrel and Peter Dimble continued to meet after work in the Iron Duke. Obviously, they wondered what had happened to their friend Archie, and they speculated, half joking, that he had fallen foul of their fiery Indian visitor. Imagine their concern, therefore, when Mr Khan reappeared.

'If you have hearts that feel, once again I beg of you, in the name of Allah and all that is holy and sacred, please sell that ring to me,' he roared, not caring who else heard him.

Once again, the clerks said they would consider his appeal, and once again they rejected it. When Khan heard this second rebuttal, Petrel said the man's long fingers twitched at his side 'like he wanted to take out a great knife and cut our guts out'. The man's face, the clerk went on, 'was all evil. For all his fine talk, I reckon he weren't no better than one of them Thuggees.'

Peter Dimble did not appear in the office the next morning. Around noon, a boatman spotted his body washed up on the right bank of the Thames at Greenwich. His throat had been cut. His pockets contained coins to the value of two shillings and fourpence halfpenny, a pencil, a handkerchief, the key to his lodgings, and the label off a beer bottle. It was a case of murder by person or persons unknown, the police told the newspapers.

Of all Peter's friends and relations, only Elijah Petrel knew of a possible suspect or motive for the killing. He was too frightened to reveal what he knew to the police, for when he had arrived home on the day Peter's body was discovered, he found on his doormat a note written in blue pencil on the back of a beer bottle label. It read:

MEET LONDON BRIGE TO-MOROW NIGHT 3 AM.
RING FOR CASH. IF TELL POLICE OR PALS YOU
DIE LIK THEM!!

After a sleepless night, the terror-stricken Petrel had gone straight to see Sherlock Holmes.

The detective read the note carefully and asked Petrel to repeat his story, paying particular attention to the words spoken by all the characters involved. He then assured the clerk that his life was almost certainly not in danger, and went to call on the pawnbroker.

Holmes asked the man behind the counter if, after he had sold the ring to the three clerks, anyone else had come in asking about it. Indeed, they had, the man replied. Strangely enough, two men who wanted the ring had been in the shop at the same time. The first was the man who had pawned it, an old soldier of rough appearance and manner who gave his name as Corporal Blanket. He had flown into a rage, swearing and cursing in the foulest language when he learned the period for redeeming the item had passed and it had been sold.

At that moment, a second man entered and enquired about the ring. Blanket withdrew into a corner and appeared to become engrossed in a display of gold watches.

The new arrival was a polite, well-spoken Indian gentleman. However, he too became deeply distressed on hearing the ring had been sold. Having pulled himself together, he asked if he might know who had bought the jewel. The pawnbroker said he didn't know the names of the three young men, but they were all clerks at the solicitor's further along the street, two houses down from the Iron Duke. The Indian thanked him and left the shop.

All this while, the old soldier had not moved.

'Had he heard what passed between yourself and the Indian?' Holmes asked.

'Almost certainly, sir.'

'And how did he react?'

'By the time the Indian gentleman had left, Corporal Blanket had calmed down. He stood looking at the floor for a few moments, muttering to himself, then walked out of the shop and went off in the same direction as the Indian.'

Holmes thanked the pawnbroker for his assistance and returned home to spend the rest of the day poring over his scrapbook of newspaper cuttings relating to crimes committed in British territories overseas. After breakfast the following day, he called at the office where Elijah Petrel worked and asked to see the ring. He examined it carefully, replaced it in the office safe, and made his way to Scotland Yard. Corporal Gulliver Blanket, formerly of the Seventeenth Foot, was arrested that afternoon and charged with the murders of Peter Dimble and Archie Falk.

What had Holmes told his friends at Scotland Yard that led to Blanket's arrest?

THE ADVENTURE OF
OLD DODSON

'That must have been the easiest piece of detective work ever undertaken,' observed Holmes at the conclusion of 'The Adventure of Old Dodson'. 'Why the officer needed to bring me in is beyond comprehension. Good heavens, Watson, even you could have solved it in a trice!'

'Old Dodson' was an elderly and none too sharp Scotland Yard detective who clung precariously to his position through the generosity of his mother-in-law's contributions to the Liberal Party. Holmes's attention was drawn to the case in question when the detective sergeant appeared at the famous Baker Street address shortly after nine o'clock one July evening. Hot, out of breath and extremely flustered, he apologized for calling at such a late hour, but feared he would lose his job unless Holmes could help him.

Holmes later confessed to Watson that he had been sorely tempted not to assist – Dodson's removal from the front line would have helped no end in the battle against crime. But Holmes was an honourable man and could not bring himself to abandon a colleague in need. With a deep sigh, he settled down and asked Dodson to explain what was troubling him.

The case was relatively simple. It concerned the murder of Miss Fanny Hogarth, a young lady from Blackheath who had been discovered by her maid with her throat cut at 7 a.m. that morning. The police had found two items of interest in her villa. The first was a jewellery box, the lid of which had been forced open and the contents removed. The second was a series of letters written by Miss Hogarth to a

certain Octavius Cannizzaro. Claiming that she was 'with child' and that Cannizzaro was the father, the letters were an attempt at blackmail: if he did not pay her the £1,000 he had promised, she would bring a suit of paternity against him.

On this evidence, Dodson concluded, there were two explanations for the murder: either an act of desperation by a robber caught in the act of stealing Miss Hogarth's jewels, or Cannizzaro ensuring his mistress's silence without having to spend a farthing. Further evidence inclined the detective towards the latter.

Octavius Cannizzaro was well known to Scotland Yard – and, it turned out, to Sherlock Holmes. He was a sinister, shadowy figure who never remained in one place long enough for the police to pin anything on him. He was rumoured to have a house and family in Luxembourg, and to make huge sums of money dealing in armaments and opium.

He travelled with no servants, rented discreet private apartments by the day when in London, and appeared to be in possession of at least three passports of different nationalities. His one weakness, if it could so be called, was for fine food. He was known in all the capital's best restaurants, both as a connoisseur of the finest wines and as a leaver of extraordinarily generous tips.

Neighbours reported having seen a man fitting Cannizzaro's description going in and out of the Blackheath villa several times over the past few days. But as the figure was hatted and heavily cloaked, even in the hottest weather, it was impossible to be certain of his identity. He had, however, been noticed leaving the villa at 6.30 a.m. that very morning. As Miss Hogarth had been dead for no more than an hour when her maid found her, Dodson felt it was safe to assume that the mysterious male visitor was her killer. And the evidence pointed strongly to that man being Cannizzaro.

Dodson alerted the force, and at 7.30 p.m. that evening a constable spotted Cannizzaro entering a private apartment near Mayfair. Dodson hurried to the address and confronted his suspect. He was under investigation for murder, he warned him. Where had he been at 6 o'clock that morning?

With a display of extreme nonchalance, Cannizzaro respectfully asked the detective to stop wasting his time. He had business to attend to before catching the 10.30 p.m. boat train from Victoria station. His presence was required in Paris for a meeting with French government officials the next day.

Dodson persisted: where had Cannizzaro been at 6 o'clock that morning? The businessman gave him an exasperated look, took out his pocket book and drew from it a sheet of paper.

'And here it is,' said Dodson, taking a crumpled receipt from his pocket. 'The perfect alibi. The dratted man even had the cheek to say that, as the document was of little interest to him, I might keep it.'

Dodson passed the paper over to Holmes. At the top was printed 'Royal Buckingham Hotel' and beneath, in bold handwriting below that day's date, 'Gratefully received from Mr Octavius Cannizzaro, at six-thirty, the sum of £1 2s 6d. For breakfast.' It was signed 'Delius Graftule, waiter'.

Holmes read the receipt carefully then jumped to his feet.

'Come on, Dodson,' he cried. 'If we hurry we can get to the Royal Buckingham and then to Victoria to apprehend our villain before he catches the boat train. We may never get another chance. Come on, man!' he added, bounding out of the door. 'Your career depends on it!'

What had Holmes spotted that Dodson had missed?

THE ADVENTURE OF THE CROOKED DRAUGHTSMAN

Sherlock Holmes was highly competitive. Failure to solve a crime cast him in deepest gloom, and he particularly relished an opportunity to succeed where others had failed – especially Scotland Yard. He was presented with one such opportunity, Watson's notes tell us, in December 1905. For reasons of national security that will soon become apparent, the doctor did not write up the case until several years after its occurrence.

Holmes disliked being told what to do, but when the command came from so august a figure as Admiral of the Fleet Sir Tommy Hunter, he felt duty bound to obey. The telegram said simply:

PRESENCE REQUIRED AT ADMIRALTY 2 PM THIS AFTERNOON STOP GIVE NAME AND ASK FOR CAPTAIN HAMMOND-SMYTHE STOP YOU WILL BE ADMITTED STOP

The detective later told Watson, 'I did as requested. Captain Hammond-Smythe met me on arrival but said hardly a word as he led me through empty, silent corridors to a small room, not more than ten feet square, above Admiralty Arch. There we were shortly joined by the great admiral himself. However, instead of exuding his usual jovial bonhomie, Sir Tommy slipped sideways into the room as if entering a Soho house of ill repute. Clearly, Watson, something significant was afoot!'

Sir Tommy told Holmes that the matter about to be laid before him was of the utmost importance, importance that went beyond the national. The future of the very Empire itself might depend on the detective's ability to solve a puzzle that had foxed the best brains in the Royal Navy and Scotland Yard. The admiral could not have known the effect this statement would have on Holmes. As far as he was concerned, something even more important than the future of the British Empire was at stake: his reputation.

After checking there was no one outside the door, Sir Tommy locked it and invited Holmes to take a seat at the small table beneath the high window overlooking Trafalgar Square. The admiral sat beside him and the captain opposite. Taking over from his superior, the captain explained that, in his capacity as officer in charge of security throughout the service, he was faced with an intractable problem.

The Royal Navy's architects and draughtsmen had been working on a new warship that would change naval warfare forever. The team allocated to the project were said to have been specially chosen for their trustworthiness as well as their technical and scientific abilities. Imagine Hammond-Smythe's dismay, therefore, when an agent operating inside the embassy of a certain foreign power warned that a serious effort was being made to discover the details of the project. Indeed, the agent reported, it was possible that a spy network was already at work.

Captain Hammond-Smythe had immediately launched a bold counter-espionage offensive. His men swept into the room where the project team worked, locking the doors and searching every desk, drawing board and person. While this was happening, the captain stood at one end of the room and watched for any sign of anxiety or unusual behaviour. Only one man gave him cause for concern.

Augustus Gedge, a forty-year-old draughtsman, had been in the service for five years. In his youth he was a keen and able sportsman, excelling at cricket and rugby football. He had been given the job at the Admiralty largely on account of a glowing reference provided by Rosslyn Park Rugby Football Club's president, a close friend of Hammond-Smythe's. To the watching officer's surprise, during the security examination Gedge had been unusually abrupt and awkward when his person was searched.

Alerted by this behaviour, Hammond-Smythe carried out further discreet checks on Gedge's background. He learned that the man was running two households: unknown to his wife and family in Battersea, he also maintained a mistress and three children in Pimlico. The strain of this double life on his finances and emotional stability was considerable, making him a suitable target for any foreign power eager to pay for information about the Navy's new project. But the captain needed evidence.

Owing to an oversight, the original search of the workplace had not included the wastepaper baskets. Thirty-six hours had now elapsed since the operation began, and the contents of the baskets had long been removed and placed in a large container ready for incineration. On Hammond-Smythe's orders, his agents combed through the mountain of refuse in search of anything unusual. They found a crumpled sheet of paper bearing the following inscription:

```
ICRSRLPHHRSRLPLPMBR
OCLPOCRSRRWHRHRF
BRWRWLPOSWFRSRLP
SHLPBSWFRSRRSRLSRRS
RHLPLPSHHRFBRWICRSR
BSWFHRICHLPOSWFOSWF
LPOSWFRSRLPSHLPHRLP
SHSHHLSRHRMBRSHLPM
BRHRHRSRRWLPOCRSRL
PSHRPMBROCSHLSRHR
```

The paper was found among others from the project room, but the handwriting was unlike that of anyone working there. When the Navy's own experts and those from Scotland Yard – sworn to secrecy – failed to make head or tail of the mysterious array of letters, Captain Hammond-Smythe was at his wits' end.

As a last resort, and with great reluctance, the captain persuaded the admiral to put the matter into the hands of London's most famous private investigator.

Holmes was briefed on Gedge and what was known of the origin of the mysterious stream of letters found on the crumpled note. After staring hard at it for five minutes,

Holmes asked whether he might be allowed to take it home. Permission was denied.

'In which case, gentlemen,' he retorted somewhat testily, 'you will have to solve this problem for yourselves.'

Holmes did not, of course, mean what he said, and Watson's jottings give a fairly clear outline of subsequent events. Having memorized the cryptic message while perusing it at the Admiralty, Holmes wrote it out when he got home and worked on it over the course of the evening. He wrote out the letters in a variety of patterns but was unable to find the key to understanding what they represented. Eventually, hoping a new day would bring enlightenment, he went to bed.

He was woken around 8.30 a.m. by Watson, who dropped in after an early-morning visit to a patient living in the vicinity. The two men breakfasted together before Holmes went back to his code and Watson read the paper. Below is the doctor's unedited version of what followed.

Reading the report of England's defeat by New Zealand in the previous day's match of rugby football, I gave a small grunt of disappointment. This appeared to annoy Holmes, who looked up and asked me what had displeased me. When I explained, he scowled, and returned to his puzzle for a few seconds before asking, 'You said rugby football, Watson?'

I replied that I had.

Though Holmes had previously shown no interest in team sports, the mention of rugby football seemed to galvanize him, and he asked me to remind him of the positions the players adopted on the field. I did so, explaining that it was becoming customary for the positions also to be known by the numbers that appeared on the back of their jerseys. This excited Holmes even more, and he jotted down this table as I dictated it:

1 = left prop

2 = hooker

3 = right prop

4 = left second row

5 = right second row

6 = blind side wing forward

7 = open side wing forward

8 = middle back row

9 = scrum half

10 = fly half

11 = left wing

12 = inside centre

13 = outside centre

14 = right wing

15 = full back

'And the referee?' he asked when I had finished. 'What is on his jersey?'

'Nothing,' I replied. 'He has no number.'

'Ah! But nothing is nought – zero – isn't it?'

I said I didn't know what he was talking about, though I did understand enough mathematics to understand that nothing was indeed nought.

Holmes was too busy scribbling to reply. A few minutes later, he threw down his pencil and let out a cry of delight.

'By Jove, Watson,' he exclaimed, 'you have just saved the Empire!'

With that, he hurried down to the telegraph office and sent an invitation to Sir Tommy to meet him at his earliest convenience at 221B Baker Street where 'a most interesting message' awaited him. The admiral and Captain Hammond-Smythe were in Holmes's apartment within the hour.

What did the coded message say, and how had Holmes deciphered it?

The Adventure of the Eccentric Nephew

Sherlock Holmes, as readers of Watson's original tales will know, was a master of disguise. But disguise is no good without the ability to act. This Holmes had in abundance, and had he been born a century later he might well have made his name in Hollywood. Those who question this assertion might like to consider 'The Adventure of the Eccentric Nephew'.

It began with a casual conversation between Holmes and Inspector Lestrade of Scotland Yard. 'Bad news,' the inspector said. Charlie 'Plastic-face' Peters, the most notorious thief in the entire southern United States, was reported to have sailed for Britain at the end of the previous year. For all Lestrade knew, the infamous fraudster was probably already at work. Holmes thanked him for the information and stored it away in his extraordinarily capacious memory.

A month later, Holmes was approached by one of Lestrade's juniors, Detective Julius Turvey, for assistance with an embarrassing burglary case. It concerned the sixty-five-year-old diamond millionaire, Sir Cecil Mount, whose country retreat of Holmarsh Abbey in Shropshire had been robbed three times in as many weeks. A quantity of jewellery and Georgian silver had been taken. When the local constabulary had failed to make any progress with the case, Sir Cecil, not the most tolerant of men, had demanded that Scotland Yard take it up. Lestrade had duly dispatched Turvey to Shropshire. When he too failed to arrest anyone, the furious Sir Cecil threatened to raise the matter with his 'friends in the government'. At that point, Turvey asked Holmes for help – and the detective duly obliged.

A quick review of the facts convinced Holmes that the Holmarsh robberies were the work of someone who knew the mansion and its workings well. Accordingly, Holmes sent the millionaire a public telegram announcing that he would be arriving at the abbey the following morning to assist Turvey with his investigation. Would Sir Cecil please ensure that none of his residential staff were absent, as Holmes wished to interview them all individually?

The abbey's six full-time staff were accordingly ushered into the library, one at a time, to meet Holmes. As Watson's notes show, the detective's skilful questioning revealed a motive for theft in every one of them.

Blodwyn Jones, the young Welsh chambermaid, was sending what she could from her wages 'back 'ome to my poor family in the Brecon hills'.

Catherine ('Katie') Duggan, the parlour maid, was saving up to marry Bertie Groundwart, a local lad who was currently serving a two-year prison sentence for attempted robbery.

The fifty-five-year-old cook, Martha Tinch, was known to spend most of her salary on Napoleon brandy, to which she was particularly partial.

Gregor de Villiers, the estate chauffeur and general handyman, was a South African who had come to England to save enough for a small farm on the veldt where, he asserted, Sir Cecil was remembered as 'a proper gent'.

Nathan Hillman, the butler, was a closet communist who handed over most of his salary to the Party.

The estate secretary, Frederick Langton, had failed to keep last year's books accurately, resulting in a shortfall of several hundred pounds.

In addition to questioning the employees about their private and public lives, Holmes also quizzed them about the stolen goods. Among other things, trying to find out how the items had been disposed of, he asked what they knew of Georgian silver. The rather strange answer one of the employees gave reminded Holmes of something Inspector Lestrade had said a while back, and he decided to investigate further.

When the interviews were over, Holmes had a private meeting with Sir Cecil. He did not pass on the confidential information he had gleaned from the employees, nor did he mention the odd remark about Georgian silver, but he did ask for four further favours.

First, would Sir Cecil please ensure that Holmes's departure for London the following day was known to all his staff? He might let it be known, too, that the detective had left in a depressed state, having failed to make any further progress in the case.

Second, would Sir Cecil himself, unseen by anyone else, alter the position of the large empty trunk Holmes had seen in the stables? He would like it resting against the inside back wall of the building. Once Sir Cecil had understood that the trunk Holmes was referring to was in fact the sea chest that once belonged to Sir Cecil's father, he agreed.

Third, would Sir Cecil also see that, until further notice, a motor car was parked overnight in the stables with the luggage compartment at the rear end facing the door?

Finally, would he and Lady Mount brief their staff about the forthcoming visit of her ladyship's mentally handicapped nephew, Horatius Knebb? Horatius was not in any way dangerous, he should tell them, but could sometimes lose his temper when thwarted. Sir Cecil and his wife would be grateful, therefore, if the staff did whatever the poor fellow asked, however bizarre it might appear.

Sir Cecil thought this last request decidedly odd,

especially as, to the best of his knowledge, his wife had no relative by the name of Horatius Knebb. Nevertheless, such was Holmes's reputation, he was intrigued by the plan and agreed to go along with it.

Poor Knebb, a stooping, shambolic figure with a decidedly eccentric manner, arrived at Hereford station a week later. Gregor de Villiers collected him, and on his return to the abbey told the other staff the fellow was 'a 22-carat nutter'. Nevertheless, they did as their employer wished, faithfully obeying Knebb's strange requests during his six-night stay.

The day after Knebb's departure, Sherlock Holmes reappeared. He had, he said, further thoughts on who might have committed the robberies. Sir Cecil hoped he had, for recently a whole lot of other things had disappeared. Not valuables this time, but a series of small but useful objects: his favourite pen, a left boot, a deerstalker hat, three books from the library, an ivory-topped walking cane, and – he blushed to mention it – a pair of her ladyship's whalebone corsets.

Holmes did not appear at all surprised and bade the millionaire accompany him to the sea chest in the stables. Inside were all the missing objects, apart from the corsets. Walking round to the rear of the motor car, Holmes politely averted his eyes and opened the boot. There, neatly folded in a brown paper parcel, lay the missing corsets.

Later that day, Gregor de Villiers was arrested and charged with travelling under a forged passport and obtaining employment under false credentials. When told he might improve his chances of avoiding extradition to the United States to stand trial in Atlanta if he admitted to the theft of numerous pieces of jewellery and silver from Holmarsh Abbey, Charlie 'Plastic-face' Peters reluctantly did so. The stolen goods were recovered shortly afterwards. What happened to Peters after a spell in Shrewsbury prison, Watson did not record.

How had Holmes identified the thief?

THE CASE OF THE FROWNING LADY

Glancing through Watson's notes, we can see that his detective friend solved a good number of the cases brought before him without needing to set foot outside 221B Baker Street. The doctor chose not to work them up into stories for publication, as tales of action and conflict were much more to his readers' taste. Nevertheless, a handful of these armchair problems are sufficiently strange, and illustrate Holmes's extraordinary powers of deduction so well, that it would be a shame not to share one or two with the twenty-first-century reader.

'The Case of the Frowning Lady' is a particularly good example.

On 14 August 1889, Holmes received the visiting card of Mrs Albert Latchcombe and, having nothing better to do on a sultry summer afternoon, asked Mrs Hudson to show the lady in. A less than light tread upon the stairs heralded the entry of a stout, corseted woman of perhaps forty years of age. The doctor's jottings, in which the words 'angry', 'vain' and 'unperceptive' are underlined, suggest that the visitor's manner was as blunt as her appearance. Watson, having learned some of the arts of close observation from his friend, noted that the lady had depressions on either side of her nose, suggesting that 'she was accustomed to wearing spectacles'.

On stepping into the room, she frowned disparagingly at the bachelor décor, frowned in the direction of Holmes, and, having also frowned towards Watson, strode towards

him and addressed him as 'Mr Sherlock Holmes'. When corrected, she made no apology but stretched out her hand to a chair, sat heavily down in it, and, at Holmes's invitation, proceeded with her story.

About ten years ago, she revealed, she had met and married the twenty-five-year-old Albert Latchcombe, a lieutenant in the Indian Army at home on extended leave. She passed Holmes a photograph of a dashing young man in the uniform of the Bengal Lancers. 'It did not take a wizard,' reflected Watson in his notes, 'to see what each party brought to the relationship.' She brought the money, he the looks.

Mrs Latchcombe related how she had fallen pregnant almost immediately and remained in England, where the baby could be born in relative comfort and safety, while her husband returned to India. As an only child whose wealthy parents were both dead, she did not lack for money. Her baby – a boy whom she said was named Albert after his father – was born in a respectable nursing home, and Mrs Latchcombe took him back with her to the pleasant single-storey villa she had bought overlooking the Sussex Downs. There she awaited her husband's letters and the expected ticket to India.

Did she have a photograph of the boy? Holmes asked. After shuffling around in her handbag, Mrs Latchcombe confessed to having forgotten to bring one with her. The detective nodded and gave Watson a curious glance.

Mrs Latchcombe said that at first her husband wrote regularly. After a while, though, his stream of correspondence dwindled to an occasional trickle – and there was no ticket. To begin with, Mrs Latchcombe explained, her husband, now promoted to captain, made excuses for his failure to arrange a passage for his wife and son, but after a year he made no further mention of the matter.

One year stretched into two, three, then four. By the fifth year, the letters from India had dried up completely. In her own words, reported by Watson, Mrs Latchcombe had 'pined and pined and pined until she feared she would waste away to a nothing, a mere thread'. The physical appearance of her son, 'so terribly like his father', was more than she could stand, and she sent him to a respectable boarding school, where he was even now.

'Imagine my shock,' the lady continued, 'when last week my husband appeared unannounced on my doorstep.' He stayed just two days – long enough, she said with a purse of the lips, to find out where everything was. At first, he seemed uneasy. Then, on the evening of the second day, he announced that their marriage was over. He had fallen in love with an Indian lady who lived with him as his wife in Bangalore. Finally, Mrs Latchcombe said that Albert, before leaving the house, had 'the bare-faced impudence' to ask for his share of the wedding settlement as he was 'finding it hard to make ends meet on his meagre officer's salary'.

'I was weeping like a fountain,' Mrs Latchcombe confessed – her 'heart was as cracked as a Christmas walnut'. She refused to give him even a penny.

Captain Latchcombe promptly left the house with a look his wife described as 'intent on returning to take his revenge'.

Her intuition, she went on, was not mistaken. The following evening, as she was leaving the bathroom (she always took a bath before dinner) wearing only her dressing gown and with 'wet hair draped about her face and shoulders', she heard a noise in the drawing room. She glanced down the corridor to see a man – unmistakeably Captain Latchcombe – rifling through the upper drawers of her writing desk. It was here that she kept her engagement ring and other pieces of precious wedding jewellery, so she could gaze on them as she wrote her letters to India.

And now this man, her own husband, had the effrontery to try to steal them. She cried out and hurried down the corridor towards him. But in the time it took her to cover the twenty or so feet to the drawing-room door, the captain had gathered up his loot and was half out of the French windows on the other side of the room. The last time she saw him he was fleeing over the lawn, a pearl necklace swinging from his right hand and his left clasped tightly round what she later discovered were two rings and an emerald brooch.

When this unusual story was over, Holmes asked two
questions. First, had Mrs Latchcombe informed the police
of the incident? No, she had not. She did not wish to be the
centre of a scandal. Instead, she would pay any fee Holmes
demanded if he would track down her errant husband.
Having done so, the detective was to tell him that, to save
himself going to prison, he should 'give up the ridiculous
idea of living in sin with an Indian', hand back his wife's
jewellery, and return to live with her 'as an honest Christian'.

Holmes's second question was a factual one. How large
was her drawing room? Mrs Latchcombe, frowning at him

harder than ever, replied that it was 'of a respectable size, perhaps forty feet from the door to the French windows'.

On receiving this answer, Holmes sighed, sat back in his chair and told his visitor there was nothing he could do to help her.

'Why ever not?' she cried. 'Clearly, Mr Holmes, you are not what people say you are. Indeed, you are a fraud.'

'Those are very harsh words, madam,' Holmes replied icily. 'But I'm afraid they are more apposite to yourself than to me. I cannot help clients who do not tell the truth.'

What were Holmes's grounds for reaching this judgement?

A Case of Ignorance

In *A Study in Scarlet*, Watson lists what he calls the 'limits' of Sherlock Holmes:

1. Knowledge of Literature. -- Nil.
2. Philosophy. -- Nil.
3. Astronomy. -- Nil.
4. Politics. -- Feeble.
5. Botany. -- Variable.

In later tales, notably 'A Scandal in Bohemia' and 'The Adventure of the Lion's Mane', Watson contradicts himself by showing Holmes to be much better read than we are led to believe. Nevertheless, his reading did have limits, and nowhere were these limits more apparent than in a case known at the time as 'The Litchburn Lovers'. It concerned Minnie Dean, from the Oxfordshire village of Litchburn, and her fiancé, Ernest Pottinger. We have pieced together the story from Watson's notes and the reports of Minnie's trial in the *Oxford Times*.

Minnie's early years were marred by unhappiness and misfortune. Her father, the village schoolmaster, died when she was sixteen, leaving her to care for her bedridden mother and three younger siblings. Money was extremely short, a fact noticed by Maxwell Naysmith-Jones, the twenty-five-year-old son of the local squire.

Carefully, mixing flattery with bribery, Naysmith-Jones won Minnie's confidence. He gave the pretty girl gifts and promised even more – hinting that one day the couple might marry. The inevitable came to pass. As many in the village had warned, Minnie became pregnant and Naysmith-Jones, denying all responsibility, left for the family plantations in Jamaica. Minnie was overwhelmed with sorrow when her baby died five days after it was born.

Two years passed. During this time, Minnie's mother passed away and two of her siblings left home to make their own way in the world. When Ernest Pottinger, one of her father's former pupils and now a graduate of Oxford University, returned home to work as a lawyer in nearby Bicester, Minnie's life finally brightened. The young couple struck up a firm friendship and were often seen walking out together.

They had much in common. Both were considered more than commonly handsome, and they shared a love of the countryside and a passion for literature engendered by Minnie's scholarly father. The same gossiping neighbours who had tutted over her relationship with Naysmith-Jones now whispered of wedding bells.

At this point Naysmith-Jones returned home from the Caribbean. When Minnie refused even to recognize him, he began to spread scandalous rumours about 'the little harlot'. Leaning up against the bar of the Red Lion, he openly disparaged Minnie to anyone willing to listen. His vitriol grew more and more malicious, until he suggested – 'and no more than a suggestion, mind you' – that Minnie had killed her baby – 'out of spite because I was called away before I could make an honest woman of her'.

When Minnie wondered in desperation whether Naysmith-Jones could be arraigned for slander, Ernest ruled it out on grounds of cost; he also noted that Minnie's persecutor always slipped a crafty 'possibly' or 'it is said' into his assertions.

Defenceless against the stream of cruel innuendo, Minnie grew more and more distraught. Even Ernest's proposal of marriage and her warm-hearted acceptance failed to lift the clouds for more than a couple of days.

Then, one chilly Sunday morning, Maxwell Naysmith-Jones was found dead at the bottom of Pilcock stone quarry. He had fallen 100 feet down the sheer face of the quarry edge and broken his neck. To the police it looked like an accidental death, but the deceased's parents thought otherwise and brought in Sherlock Holmes to investigate.

Holmes uncovered a good deal of evidence. Though none of it reflected well on Naysmith-Jones, key elements of it suggested his death had not been an accident. He drank heavily on the night he died, finally staggering out of the Red Lion shortly before midnight. Several eyewitnesses, aroused by his shouting and swearing, saw him hammer on the door of Minnie's cottage, demanding to be let in. She eventually opened the door and the drunkard disappeared inside.

Joshua Plow, who lived opposite, testified that the cottage door opened fifteen minutes later, and Minnie and Naysmith-Jones emerged hand in hand. She seemed, said Joshua, 'very sweet towards him'. They walked off round the side of the house in the direction of the quarry. That was at 12.15 a.m., as confirmed by the chimes of the church clock.

The next thing Joshua saw was Ernest Pottinger running towards Minnie's cottage. Warned of Naysmith-Jones's antics by a friend, he had hurried there to check that his fiancée was all right. Joshua says Pottinger entered her cottage, calling her name before lighting a candle to search the rooms. After a while, he came out to see Minnie returning alone. The couple threw themselves into each other's arms and stood talking for some time before entering the house together. They had met just after 12.45 a.m., Joshua said, the timing again confirmed by the church clock.

What had happened between Minnie and Naysmith-Jones leaving her cottage together, and her return alone half an hour later? She said that rather than fight the drunken and angry intruder, a struggle she would inevitably have lost, she had chosen to sweet talk him into going for a walk with her. She hoped the fresh night air would sober him up sufficiently to see the error of his ways and let her go. When this did not happen, she slipped away from him in the darkness and hurried home. She had gone nowhere near the quarry.

Hurried home? asked Holmes when interviewing her. She thought for a moment then said she recalled wandering about for a while, collecting her thoughts, before returning to her cottage to find Ernest waiting for her.

Earlier that day, Holmes had walked slowly between the cottage door and the edge of the quarry. The journey there and back had taken him just under half an hour, the precise time Minnie had been absent on the night of the accident.

Holmes had one further matter to raise. On searching the quarry, he had found, near where the body had lain, a lady's hair comb hidden between the stones. Had Minnie lost such a comb?

She blushed and said she had.

Could she explain how it might have found its way into the quarry when she had not gone near the place?

She could only think that, in one of her several struggles with Naysmith-Jones that night, he had grabbed it from her head and kept it – perhaps as a memento of his past wickedness.

Or, in his state of drunken befuddlement, suggested Holmes, might he have grabbed it from her as she manoeuvred him to the edge of the quarry and pushed him off?

No! Not true! She could never do such a thing. As she had said, she had been nowhere near the quarry.

Holmes had been questioning Minnie in her cottage. As he was leaving, he met her fiancé by the garden gate. The two men exchanged a brief greeting and parted. As Ernest Pottinger continued up the garden path towards the cottage, Sherlock Holmes knelt down behind the front hedge in the pretence of doing up a bootlace. He wanted to hear how the couple greeted each other.

'Well, my darling,' he heard Ernest say as Minnie opened

the front door to him, 'I trust there'll be no Stonehenge moment for Tess of the Litchburns?'

'No, my angel,' she laughed. 'I'm much hardier than old Tom's girl, ha-ha!'

After that, they went inside and Holmes heard no more. He pondered their words for a few moments before dismissing them as the sort of intimate nonsense lovers sometimes spoke – so he had been told, anyway. He had no first-hand experience of such banalities.

Drawing on the evidence Holmes had provided, Minnie Dean was tried at Oxford Crown Court for the murder of Maxwell Naysmith-Jones. From the start, the *Oxford Times* sided strongly with a 'pretty young girl who all her life had been harassed and taken advantage of by a drunken cad', and the paper made it clear what it thought the jury should do. After twelve hours of heated deliberation, it duly obliged – Minnie Dean was found not guilty of the murder of Maxwell Naysmith-Jones.

Holmes was not surprised by the verdict, though he was convinced it was the wrong one. 'It's most unlike me, Watson,' he confessed, 'but I'm sure I overlooked some vital piece of evidence. But I'm deuced if I know what it is.'

He was right. He had missed a piece of evidence that, if presented to the jury, might well have persuaded them to return a guilty verdict.

What was it?

THE CASE OF THE
SURGEON'S SECRET

As we saw in 'The Case of the Frowning Lady', Holmes liked to solve the mysteries presented to him as swiftly as possible. The tale that follows, reconstructed from Watson's notes, is another example of the great detective resolving a client's problem without leaving Baker Street.

Early in the twentieth century, Lord Edward Frogmore, a young baronet of considerable fortune, called at Holmes's lodging in a state of some anxiety to discuss what he described as a 'deeply personal matter'. Holmes said he was not a priest but would do what he could for a fee of £500. The peer immediately wrote out a cheque for that amount and placed it on the table between himself and Holmes.

His lordship explained that, as they may have read in the papers, he was engaged to Agnes Axelson, the twenty-one-year-old daughter of Roald Axelson, a successful American manufacturer of steam locomotives. The young couple had met while she was travelling around Europe with her father. Her mother, who had remained at home to fulfil 'pressing engagements', was due to arrive at Southampton in time for the wedding, which would take place later that year at the home of Lord Frogmore's father, the Duke of Sussex.

Lord Edward loved his fiancée dearly and had every reason to believe his feelings were reciprocated. Imagine his distress, therefore, when glancing casually at the blotter upon which she had been writing a letter, he discerned the following imprint:

uoy evol syawla lliw …
… traeh ym lla htiW

The young man's quick mind immediately reversed the words to reveal their meaning:

… will always love you
with all my heart …

He resisted the temptation to question Agnes immediately, but waited until they were alone before asking, as nonchalantly as he was able, who she had been writing to.

When she replied with a gay laugh, 'Oh, just a quick note to my surgeon,' and quickly changed the subject, suspicions flooded the young peer's mind. He knew little of his fiancée's past, though he was aware that ten months previously, while she was still in the United States, she had been seriously ill with a 'private' complaint that a surgeon had treated with complete success.

Given the delicate nature of the issue, Lord Edward had not enquired further. But now ... Of course! Agnes had fallen for the dashing young surgeon who had cured her of this distressing malady. Moreover, as her complaint had obviously been gynaecological, he must have examined her most intimately. The thought fired his lordship's fertile imagination to conjure up lascivious images of Agnes with her surgeon. The relationship explained why she was in Europe, too: her father must have disapproved of the match and brought her across the Atlantic to get away from her seducer. But the plan had failed, hadn't it? She would always love her surgeon, and had said as much in black and white.

Breaking off the engagement would make him a laughing stock and bring shame on himself and his family, concluded Lord Frogmore. But what else was there to do?

As the peer was talking, Holmes had taken down a scrapbook of newspaper cuttings and checked an entry entitled 'Scalpels and Skirts: Modern Medicine the American Way'. He still had the cutting before him when his client finished his story.

'Would you be so good as to remind me of your fiancée's name, sir?' he asked, keeping his finger on a line in the article.

'Miss Agnes Axelson.'

'And the spelling of the surname?'

'A X E L S O N.'

'In which case,' said Holmes, rising and replacing the scrapbook back on the shelf, 'it's very clear to me what you should do.' He moved back to the table and picked up the cheque made out in his name.

Lord Frogmore leaned forwards anxiously. 'And that is, Mr Holmes?'

'Carry on exactly as you were before the unfortunate incident of the blotting paper. You have nothing to fear from the surgeon, I assure you.'

How could Holmes have been so certain?

THE ADVENTURE OF THE ARCHWAY OPERATOR

O ne of the last cases recorded in Watson's notes involved the criminal fraternity's use – or misuse – of the rapidly expanding telephone system. It centred around a series of daring bank raids in and around London's Highgate Archway during the summer of 1911.

In broad daylight, three masked men, armed with heavy pistols, forced their way into branches of the Westminster, National Provincial and Lloyds banks. After terrifying staff and customers by firing several pistol shots, shooting dead a customer in one raid and seriously injuring a teller in another, the gang threatened to kill everyone in the building unless 'all the cash you've got' was handed over. In every instance, they left with over £10,000 stuffed into a large leather holdall.

The Metropolitan Police scoured the underworld in vain for information that might identify the robbers – those who in normal circumstances might have grassed in exchange for a reward kept their mouths tightly shut for fear of reprisal. Whoever the 'Archway Gang' (as they were known in the press) were, they were certainly ruthless.

The bravery of a passer-by finally brought the raids to an end. Standing by the door of a branch of Lloyds Bank as the thieves were running out with their loot, the man made a grab at the mask of the last one to leave. The knotted red handkerchief fell away to reveal the unmistakable face of Jo Yendle, a notorious criminal who had twice before been imprisoned for theft. The rogue turned and beat his assailant to the ground with his pistol. He would almost

certainly have killed him had not a crowd gathered and forced Yendle to the pavement, where he was held until the arrival of the police. In the meantime, the other two members of the gang had made their getaway in a stolen motor car.

Though charged with murder in addition to other offences, Yendle refused to reveal the names of the two members of his gang who had escaped. The only item of interest in his possession when arrested was a notebook. It contained several dates and hastily scribbled figures in what was identified as Yendle's handwriting. One page seemed of particular interest. Under the heading 'Agreement' was a series of telephone numbers with percentage signs beneath them:

HAMPSTEAD	847
ABBEY	758
MOORGATE	212
PADDINGTON	887
DILIGENCE	001
EDGWARE	666
NATIONAL	992
= 30%	= 15%

When the police asked the operator to call these numbers, they were told either that the number did not exist, or that, where it was genuine, the subscriber clearly had no link to criminal activity.

In the end, the detectives working on the case took the notebook to Sherlock Holmes in the hope that he could work out what the numbers meant. Within twenty minutes he had revealed the names of the two missing members of the Archway Gang.

Who were they?

SOLUTIONS

The Mystery of Baron Galtür

Holmes's suggestions to Baron Galtür's Viennese lawyer ran as follows:

1. Check the size of shoe worn by the baron and the two von Wasptakkers; Holmes suspected they were either exactly the same or that George's feet were slightly smaller than those of the other two men. This would allow him to wear their shoes.

2. Ask the local policeman, the innkeeper and the detectives whether they had inspected the eaves of the inn at any point during the five days of very cold weather that had followed the night of the murder. Had they noticed a large icicle broken off near the window of Egmont's bedroom? If they had, then there was the murder weapon – not the bayonet from the great hall.

3. Either question George von Wasptakker himself, if possible, or re-read very carefully the transcript of the detectives' interview with him. Egmont had declared his brother to be more in love with Elizabeth than he was – how would such an earnest, passionate young man react when he learned that his beloved had been seduced by a heartless philanderer, even though that philanderer were his own brother?

4. Ask the landlord and other staff at the inn about the relationship between the two von Wasptakker brothers. Had they always been on the best of terms? Had they argued? If so, what about?

The Viennese lawyer, having done as Holmes suggested, was able to present the court with a most plausible alternative account of the events of the night of the murder. Having learned of his brother's behaviour towards Elizabeth, a girl he worshipped with a chaste passion, the heartbroken George von Wasptakker was smitten with jealous fury. When he heard the baron say he would kill Egmont, he persuaded himself that the deed should be done by himself to atone for this brother's wickedness and protect what remained of his beloved's honour. He planned, once Egmont was out of the way and the baron either hanged or imprisoned for life, to marry Elizabeth himself and care for the child she was carrying.

The first step was to slay Egmont.

George had stabbed his brother in the neck with a large icicle he took from outside the sleeping youth's bedroom window. One blow was sufficient, after which he held the weapon before the bedroom fire, melting it to water, which doused the flames.

The second step was to incriminate the baron. To do this, George took the key to the castle from Egmont's pocket, put on his brother's boots and walked across the fresh snow to the servants' door of the castle. Having let himself in, he slipped out of his brother's boots and put on a pair of the baron's that had been left out for cleaning. After wiping one of the bayonets hanging in the great hall, George left the castle through the front door, walked across to the inn and then returned to the castle. Clear footprints now appeared to show the baron walking to the inn and back.

All George had to do now was return the baron's boots to the place where he had found them, get back into the boots of his dead brother, return to the inn, and go back to bed. The trap was sprung. In the morning, he would feign horrified surprise at the discovery of his brother's body, and puzzlement at the footprints in the snow and the clean bayonet. Then, of course, he would remember the baron saying he would kill Egmont …

Though the lawyer managed to get the baron acquitted, it was left to George to confirm his guilt. He did so by writing a full confession, then shooting himself one afternoon in the Viennese woods. The act confirmed Holmes's interpretation of the case – and earned him five guineas from a profoundly impressed Dr Watson.

The Adventure of the *Adelaide Star*

Holmes, ever curious about the workings of the criminal mind, was suspicious from the moment he heard Mrs

Thriepland's story of sudden death, burial at sea, and theft. Such a strange coincidence of circumstances was hard to credit.

The telegram supposedly sent by Mr Thriepland to his on-board mistress added to Holmes's misgivings. Why send a telegram when he could deliver the message verbally, in person? Perhaps the message asked the young woman to speak only with her eyes because she could not discourse openly with the sender? If that was the case, then the 'Teddy' of the telegram was not Mr Edward Thriepland. And was the gritty tycoon really the type to make oblique, semi-poetic references ('brilliant eyes' and 'future gleams') to his mistress's good looks? Wasn't the language more likely to be a deliberate but oblique reference to the diamonds? The quote from *Macbeth* ('Leave all the rest to me'), relating to a proposed murder, was especially suspicious.

The situation became clearer at Hatton Garden, where Holmes learned about the man from the colonies wanting to sell uncut diamonds. If these were indeed the Thriepland jewels, then the false wife had not been acting alone. Was her accomplice the mysterious 'Teddy' of the telegram?

Holmes's visit to the offices of O & C drew the net tighter. Dr Hogwin E. Palfrey, the locum doctor who had come on board the *Adelaide Star* at short notice, had the middle name of Edward.

198

'Had you been baptized "Hogwin", my dear Watson, wouldn't you have chosen to use your middle name?' remarked Holmes on returning to Baker Street.

The interviews with Captain Penprase and Nancy Denne completed Holmes's picture of the whole murderous plot. Dr Palfrey was a cold-hearted villain prepared to do anything to become rich. His girlfriend, Emma Trowbridge, a secretary at Colonial Gems, Melbourne, was madly in love with him and also desirous of wealth. At Palfrey's request, she became the mistress of her boss, Edward Thriepland, and inveigled him into getting her a false passport and taking her with him to England as Mrs Thriepland. To be on the UK-bound liner with her, Palfrey incapacitated the ship's doctor with a mild dose of poison and took his place on board.

Now the false Mrs Thriepland and Dr Palfrey were together, they acted in concert to do away with their target and steal his diamonds. Holmes saw through the doctor's diagnosis of 'heart attack' straight away: myocardial infarction invariably produces sweating, while the captain said Mr Thriepland's skin was dry; furthermore, the patient attempted to summon the stewardess with his left arm, a limb incapacitated by a heart attack. Holmes also noted how strange it was for the doctor to have had his bag ready by the door when Nancy, the stewardess, summoned him. It was almost as if he knew what was going to happen.

To the world's leading expert on poisons, the fact that Nancy found Dr Palfrey eating almond-smelling macaroons clinched the matter: Holmes immediately identified the distinct odour of potassium cyanide. The macaroons were merely a misdirection to cover the smell. It was this drug, not morphine, that Dr Palfrey had injected into Mr Thriepland – and the dose had proved fatal. The man's violent stomach pains earlier that evening were probably due to the ingestion of some milder poison slipped into his afternoon tea by his mistress. The substance was doubtless provided by the doctor and may well have been the same as that used to incapacitate the ship's real doctor back in Melbourne.

Holmes had to admit that burial at sea was 'a touch of evil genius'. The detective could have Dr Palfrey and his accomplice charged with the theft of the diamonds, but evidence of their participation in a much more serious crime lay at the bottom of the South Atlantic.

As is so often the case, however, the criminal overreached himself. By setting up home with Emma Trowbridge, Dr Palfrey believed he could guarantee her silence. But when she confessed to being stricken with guilt at what she had done, he determined to get rid of her. Poison was again his preferred method, but this time administered over a period of weeks.

Examining Emma's body when he called in at the local undertaker, Holmes found it contaminated by arsenic. He also recovered the Thriepland diamonds from a safe in the doctor's cellar. As a consequence, Dr 'Teddy' Palfrey was found guilty of theft and a single charge of murder. Holmes remained convinced it should have been a double charge.

The Mystery of the Stabbed Shakespearean

The lack of rouge on the rim of either of the glasses found in Professor Thomas's room immediately made Holmes wary of suspecting Hélène La Chaise of murder. Moreover, the use of a knitting needle, if that was indeed the murder weapon, would imply premeditation – so why the loud argument and strange choice of weapon?

Hélène might have had a motive for wanting Thomas silenced, but so did Wynberg. Both had a reputation to save.

Holmes's alternative interpretation of the overheard words was as follows:

'Helen' was not the professor's mistress but 'the face that launched a thousand ships' in Christopher Marlowe's play *Doctor Faustus*. 'Debt' was in fact the first syllable of 'Deptford', where Marlowe was murdered. 'Butter' – or more accurately 'but a' – linked neatly to Wynberg's 'I spy my foot' utterance. When Thomas referred to Marlowe as 'nothing *but a* spy', the taunt had goaded the drunken

American into murder. Afterwards, still befuddled by alcohol, he continued to refute the gibe. But his words – 'A spy? My foot!' – had been misheard by the porter.

And the murder weapon? The golden quill. Drunk and taunted beyond breaking point by scholarly darts, Wynberg had drawn the instrument from his pocket and stabbed Thomas in the eye, repeating the manner of Marlowe's death in a pub in Deptford in 1593. The Oxford detective, armed with a lens borrowed from Sherlock Holmes, found suspicious traces of a red-brown substance inside the quill. Holmes's pioneering chemical knowledge proved these to be human blood.

Faced with such overwhelming evidence against him, Wynberg confessed his guilt and was sent for trial at the Oxford assizes.

The Lady from Kent

A series of inconsistencies and suspicions caused Holmes's misgivings about Mrs Elizabeth Flowers' story.

First, the stain on her boot, which Watson mistook for a scald. Holmes correctly interpreted it as a chemical burn. What, he wondered, was she doing with chemicals when she had not worked in Gregory Flowers' laboratory for, what, several years?

Second, her behaviour. Her hysterical crying was too convincing to be real, and Holmes suspected theatrical training. This tied in with his doubts about the black circles under her eyes. He himself was an expert in disguise and make-up, and when she took great care not to smudge the marks when drying her tears, he was convinced they were the product of greasepaint rather than insomnia. She also drew attention to her theatrical background when she used the expression 'stage left' while explaining the position of Wincott Flowers' wine glass.

Third, 'the lady doth protest too much', as Watson quoted in his notes. If the case against Gregory Flowers was so obvious, why not go to the police? Or at least discuss it with her husband: the excuse about not wanting 'to alarm him unduly' was ridiculously flimsy. By pointing the finger so vehemently at Gregory, Elizabeth Flowers employed an old trick that Holmes saw through almost immediately.

Fourth, if she had really caught a train from Tunbridge Wells to Victoria around noon and had come directly to Baker Street – as she said she had done – she would have arrived in the early afternoon. In fact, she had arrived as it was getting dark. Where, Holmes wondered, had she been in the intervening hours?

Fifth, the cab that brought her to Baker Street had come from the north. The fact that Watson saw Holmes lit by the setting sun as he entered his friend's sitting room reminds us that his rooms at 221B faced west, on the same side of the street as traffic heading south. Holmes saw her cab draw up alongside the pavement before she alighted adjacent to his house; in other words, she had been travelling from north to south. She said she had come directly from Victoria station, to the south of Baker Street. This was a lie. Had she really been going north, she would have stopped on the other side of the street and needed to cross the road to 221B.

Finally, Holmes's acute sense of smell, carefully trained, had picked up the smell of cigarette smoke on her clothing. This in itself was sufficient to fuel his growing suspicions. Later, he explained to the police that he had even been able to identify the tobacco – a rare blend sold only by a tobacconist in Swiss Cottage. Since neither she nor Edward smoked, and the chance of her having travelled on a train with someone smoking these most unusual cigarettes was minimal, Holmes deduced that in all likelihood she had come not from Victoria station but from an assignation with someone from the north London district of Swiss Cottage who smoked cigarettes.

The smell of tobacco on Mrs Flowers' clothing, her arrival in a cab from north London, and her failure to account for the missing hours on the afternoon of her visit to Baker Street all suggested to Holmes that the lady may well have had an amorous as well as financial motive for wishing her husband out of the way.

The detective presented his suspicions to Scotland Yard without delay. Swift investigations revealed that Elizabeth

Flowers did indeed have a lover living in north London. His name was William Gramolt, a man she had known from her teenage days in the theatre. The pair later confessed to having concocted an elaborate plot to rob the Flowers family of their fortune.

The first step had been for Elizabeth to wheedle her way into Gregory Flowers' laboratory, where she learned about poisons. The job also brought her into contact with Edward, whom she admitted to having seduced into marriage by telling him she was pregnant. She was not – her admission of childlessness after five years of marriage was another reason Holmes suspected her union with Edward was not as loving as she had pretended it to be on her visit to Baker Street.

The last stage of the evil intrigue involved poisoning Edward, leaving his wife to inherit his fortune and positioning Gregory as the prime suspect. The criminal couple did not really care whether the fellow went to the gallows as long as attention was diverted from themselves.

Approaching Sherlock Holmes to warn of Edward's impending death was a clever but dangerous tactic. In employing it, Elizabeth seriously underestimated the detective's abilities: instead of shifting the spotlight of suspicion on to Gregory, she succeeded only in swinging it round to shine fully on herself.

Watson's notes do not tell us what befell Elizabeth Flowers and William Gramolt in the end, although we can probably guess.

The final word in this classic case comes from Sherlock Holmes himself. At the foot of his notes on 'The Lady from Kent', Watson wrote:

On the way back to Baker Street in a cab, I asked my friend what his latest adventure had taught him.

'Nothing at all, my dear Watson,' he replied, 'though it did reinforce one of my golden rules.'

'Ah! May I ask what that rule is?'

Holmes paused for a second for the vestige of a smile to pass across his thin lips. 'Sadly, it's something you and your fellow romantics will not be able to follow, Watson: never, under any circumstances whatsoever, allow a pretty face to divert you from the path of reason.'

The Case of the Enamel Brooch

When Emily de Chablis implored Holmes to reveal more of her lineage, a strange look came over the detective's face. After giving her another searching look, he stared up at the ceiling, then down at his feet. Watson could not believe it: for a good minute, Sherlock Holmes was lost for words!

When he finally spoke, it was 'in an oddly reserved manner, as if the words were being squeezed out of him like juice from a lemon'. He began by saying that he recalled the case of the murder of M. Édouard de Chablis, having read about it in the French press. He coughed before going on. The unfortunate gentleman had been shot dead by communists for no other reason than that he was a close confidant of Louis-Philippe Albert d'Orléans, Count of Paris, whom French royalists believed to be the rightful King of France. Some said – and again Holmes gave a nervous cough – that Édouard de Chablis was in fact related to the count. In other words, he had royal blood.

The news delighted Miss de Chablis. She felt it explained the priceless jewel and why her mother had fled to England in distress, fearing herself to be next on the assassins' list. 'And I may tell my future father-in-law that, according to no lesser a person than the great Mr Sherlock Holmes, I most probably have royal blood in my veins?' she asked as she rose to leave.

Holmes nodded. 'Indeed, you may, Miss de Chablis. Indeed, you may.'

The moment the door closed behind her, Holmes muttered, 'Well, I was only half lying, wasn't I, Watson? Poor thing! It is not for us to break her heart, reveal her illegitimacy, and place her at the centre of a national scandal, wouldn't you agree?'

The doctor was mystified. Watson wrote that Holmes let out an exasperated sigh and wondered how someone so poor at interpreting evidence ever made a correct medical diagnosis. He then explained his conclusion.

His suspicions had been aroused immediately he set eyes on the young woman. Unlike Watson, he realized at once whom she resembled. The brooch and her age confirmed it. 'Chab' was not short for Chablis but for Le Chabanais, the most famous brothel in Paris, an institution patronized by statesmen and royalty alike. Liza Wilkins may have earned her living by teaching during her stay in Paris, but her lessons were not in English grammar. Édouard de Chablis, blue blooded or not, had never existed: the 'de Chablis' title and 'Édouard', the French version of the father's first name, were fictions created to give respectability to her pregnancy.

The name 'Edward' on the brooch was not an anglicized version of Édouard, but the real name of the donor of the jewel: Prince Edward, the eldest son of Queen Victoria. A well-known frequenter of the five-star brothel at the time of Emily de Chablis' conception, the Prince – 'du [of the] Chabanais' – had in all likelihood given the enamel brooch to Liza Wilkins as a mark of royal gratitude for services rendered.

And Emily de Chablis' physical appearance? When Watson protested that she was not at all like Prince Edward, the future Edward VII, Holmes almost shouted with exasperation. 'No, my dear Watson! The girl does not resemble her father, but her grandmother. Can't you see? She is the spitting image of the young Victoria.'

Watson did not record his reaction to this news, though

the PS label he gave the case explains why he thought it best for all concerned if it remained within the walls of 221B Baker Street.

The Mystery of the Fourth Trombone

'The Mystery of the Fourth Trombone' is an unusual example of Holmes using his musical knowledge in the pursuit of justice.

Holmes's misgivings had been raised by the coincidence of a number of factors. The first was de Mainville's sudden absence from the orchestra. This by itself was not suspicious, but became so when taken alongside other strange goings on.

One of these was Horváth's placing of a pocket watch on the lectern beside the score. Holmes, who had never seen or heard of this before, was immediately curious as to its purpose. The situation became a little clearer when the conductor began inserting random *rallentandos* and *accelerandos* into the music, as Holmes noticed when he attempted and failed to beat time with his fingers. The orchestra's puzzlement confirmed that something unusual was going on. The only explanation, as Holmes muttered to Watson at the time, was that Horváth was steering the overture according to a strict chronological timetable.

The detective had no idea why this should be until he learned of de Mainville's death by gunshot while the Tchaikovsky overture was at its most deafening. The fourth trombone's suicide at that precise moment might have been a most extraordinary coincidence – but surely not when the conductor had engineered the music so that it would be certain to drown out what was going on in the Green Room.

The Metropolitan Police, alerted by Holmes, carried out a thorough investigation into de Mainville's death and, as the detective feared, uncovered a heinous plot.

Oskar Horváth turned out to be an addicted gambler as well as a brilliant musician. De Mainville was a lesser musician but, as the only son of a prominent banker, a great deal wealthier. Horváth had privately borrowed huge sums from him. When the maestro failed to repay his debts and the trombonist threatened to go public, the desperate conductor used his last remaining pounds to hire the services of a hitman.

Horváth and the assassin drew up what they hoped would be a foolproof plan. The conductor paid a failed doctor, eager to earn a few guineas, to provide a substance that would make the trombonist suddenly and violently unwell. The assassin then joined the Hall's catering staff under an assumed name, put the toxin into a sandwich, and fed it to his victim in the break between the cantata and the overture. As the other players were returning to the stage, de Mainville offered hasty apologies, headed straight for the lavatories and was violently ill. The killer waited until the Green Room was empty, then followed him there. As the timpani boomed overhead, at precisely 5.43 p.m., he shot him dead and laid the murder weapon beside the body.

The police's suspicion of suicide, perhaps as a result of depression intensified by severe gastric influenza, was set aside, and the law took its inexorable course with Horváth and his accomplice.

'The timing of the two men was spot on,' remarked Holmes wryly as he and Watson talked over the case a few weeks later. 'With one exception.'

'Oh yes?'

'It was not very clever to plan the murder for a concert at which I was present, was it, Watson?'

The Mystery of the Strangled Poet

Holmes had dismissed Lord Abbas as a suspect the moment he met him. Only a man of considerable subtlety would have risked hiring a detective to solve a crime he himself had committed. Given the lack of evidence of a break-in, therefore, the murder must have been committed by someone from Cranmer House. Fawcett's pederastic behaviour was an obvious motive, and Holmes admitted that this had indeed sidetracked him for a while.

211

His interview with the matron, Mrs Mussett, had brought him back on to the right path. An alluring widow who loved every minute of her time at Cranmer House; an extremely attractive young man who came to her complaining of heartburn; a homosexual poet who ranted against the 'storm' going on above him and decided to betray what he abhorred. The picture was not hard to imagine.

Both guilty parties made serious errors during their interviews with Holmes. In a strictly 'surnames only' house, Mrs Mussett had repeatedly referred to the Head of House as 'Sebastian'. And on a tempestuous night when he was supposed to have been in his bed in the south-west-facing dormitory, Crawley said he had heard the clock strike twelve-thirty: he could have done so only if he had been near an open window on the leeward side of the building facing the church, so loud was the wind. As the doors to the kitchen were locked, the young man must have been in Fawcett's study at the time he was strangled.

In the matron's rooms Granger found two ferry tickets from Weymouth to Barfleur. Hearing from Wray that Lord Abbas had employed the services of the celebrated Sherlock Holmes, Mrs Mussett, on the morning of his arrival, had gone to Weymouth not to visit her sister but to buy the tickets. She had planned to elope to France with her young lover the following evening.

Upon the discovery of the tickets, the matron confessed to plotting to run away with Sebastian Crawley. It was a love affair and nothing else, she insisted, and had nothing to do with the unfortunate death of poor Fawcett. Her paramour was less sanguine. Faced with overwhelming circumstantial evidence against him, Crawley broke down under police questioning.

Desperately trying to avoid the gallows, he blamed everything on Sophia Mussett. She had seduced him four weeks earlier, he said, and when their noisy lovemaking was interrupted by Fawcett on the night of the storm, she had begged him to silence the man before he made their relationship public and ruined them both. Suspicion, she added, would surely fall on Lord Abbas, whose threats against Fawcett were common knowledge. In thrall to her beauty, Crawley had followed the house tutor back downstairs and strangled him in his own study.

'Rum old business,' muttered Lord Abbas as he handed Holmes a cheque for the second half of his fee. 'No accounting for what chaps'll get up to when the old heart starts thumping, eh?'

Holmes did not reply.

The Adventure of the Axelbury Arsonist

The investigation into the theft of the Teasebury necklace had been handled by the Somerset constabulary. Their efforts had proved fruitless, though they were convinced it had been the work of Piccard Grantham. After his arrest and conviction on another charge, therefore, they chose to let the matter rest until his release from prison. They would then keep him under surveillance and let him lead them to wherever he had hidden the necklace.

'If only they had asked the right questions at the time of the robbery,' Holmes grumbled, 'there would have been no need for us to waste time travelling to Somerset.'

Watson chose to ignore the second part of his friend's statement, and asked what those 'right questions' were.

There were four, said Holmes. One, how did the thief know that the house's occupants were distracted, thus allowing him to enter? Two, was it purely by chance he found Miss Teasebury's bedroom and knew exactly what he was looking for and where to find it? Three, would a man who had never driven a motor car and had little idea how to do so try to get away in a hurry by driving one? Fourth, if the intruder was not trying to start the motor, what was he doing beside the vehicle?

Even before he left London, Holmes had decided the thief must have been assisted by someone within the Hall – how else would they have known the necklace's precise location? When he heard about the trips to Shepton Mallet, the town where Grantham was incarcerated, he narrowed down the suspects to two: Hazelhurst the chauffeur and Molly the maid.

Holmes had considered early on that the motor car might be linked to the theft – it was suspicious that two major crimes had occurred in the same place within months of each other – but he was not sure how. The conversations with Hazelhurst and the cab driver, revealing the slight differences in method between the Axelbury fire-raising and the other four arson cases, suggested to Holmes that the latter incident was the work of a different criminal from the previous four. (This was proved to be correct when, a week later, an aggrieved blacksmith from Kingston St Mary was caught in the act of trying to set fire to a garage by placing a flaming hay bale before its doors.)

If the Axelbury arsonist was a copycat villain, using the previous cases as a cover, who were they and why did they want the Buick destroyed?

Hazelhurst was the obvious suspect because he had full access to the motor car and the garage. Moreover, Holmes's examination of the burned-out vehicle provided a possible motive. The chauffeur had reported Grantham, now in jail, as trying to start the Buick on the evening of the theft. In fact, Holmes had realized, Grantham had been dropping the stolen necklace in its fuel tank. Hazelhurst may have seen this and used the car's destruction to hide his hacking into the fuel tank to recover the jewellery for himself. Alternatively, he may have committed the theft and invented his sighting of Grantham as a diversion. But why conceal the necklace in a fuel tank? And why recover it by destroying the car when he could easily have worked on the fuel tank without arousing suspicion?

No, Holmes decided, Hazelhurst was not the villain he was looking for.

That left Grantham and his accomplice. At some stage the former crab fisherman had probably told his partner in crime where he had hidden his loot, though for a while neither of them could work out how to get it back. Then came the arson attacks. Grantham learned about them from his accomplice during a visit to Shepton Mallet prison and together they devised a plan to hide the recovery of the necklace by setting fire to the Buick.

Following this line of reasoning, Holmes was fairly sure that Grantham's accomplice had to be his secret sweetheart Molly. She would have known where the necklace was kept and could have directed Grantham there on an evening when she was certain the household would be preoccupied with the dinner party.

But Holmes needed proof of his hypothesis. A necklace that had lain for weeks in a fuel tank would surely give off at least a faint whiff of petrol. The cold, which had made Watson so anxious, was merely an excuse for Holmes to sniff carefully in every room he entered when interviewing the staff. In Molly's he caught the unmistakable smell of petrol that still lingered on the stolen jewellery.

He confirmed his supposition by telephoning the governor of Shepton Mallet jail and learning that a certain Molly Fish had visited Piccard Grantham twice in the last month.

Watson concludes his notes by remarking that, contrary to what Holmes had said, the trip to Somerset had not been a waste of time, for anyone. Constable Diggins had got his man, or rather his woman; Agatha Teasebury had got her necklace back; Holmes had received a cheque for £750; and Watson had met face to face with the Dove of Drury Lane.

The Mystery of the Early Cuckoo

Holmes had been intrigued by a number of issues in Lilly Phillips' story. He was unconvinced by Gustav Strauss's reason for refusing to marry. A possible explanation, he surmised, was that the man did not wish to reveal his real name, something he would have had to do for a marriage to be legal.

The name puzzle deepened when Holmes learned that letters from abroad (almost certainly Switzerland) were addressed to 'Sauber-Strauss'. As the sender had hyphenated the name of the clock (which Strauss claimed to have been that of his mother) with that of the inventor, the author may well have been one of Strauss's Sauber relations.

What had prompted this person to write? The fact that they did so shortly after the publication of the article in the *Illustrated London News* was surely telling. But what might the letter contain? A begging missive was an obvious explanation, but that would not have prompted the recipient's alarmed and secretive reaction. No, whoever wrote those letters included information – or made demands – that caused Strauss (if that were his real name) much distress.

Having got this far in the case, Holmes considered the other pieces of evidence. First, the sudden arrival and peculiar behaviour of the French tinker. Several things struck the detective as worthy of note: the man's appearance had coincided with the mysterious early cuckoo sounds; he was in the Brickmaker's Arms on the evening when the maid's house key (but not a substantial sum of money) had been stolen; he had left the district immediately after Strauss's murder; as a speaker of *Schweizerdeutsch*, he was probably Swiss, not French; he was neither as poor (he was wearing a silver watch chain) nor as short-sighted as he professed to be. All of these facts, Holmes knew, proved nothing, but they did confirm that the man was a fraud who was likely to be linked in some way to Strauss's death. He was possibly the inventor's Swiss correspondent, too.

Holmes now focused his thoughts on the unlocked bureau and on the prototype cuckoo clock that had fallen into the bath. As Lilly had not seen a clock of that type before, the chances were it had been brought into the house while she was away. By whom? And why? The answer to the first may well have been the false tinker. Perhaps his reason for doing so lay in the fruitless search through the bureau?

Summarizing his deductions thus far, Holmes decided it most likely that the intruder, probably the tinker, had stolen the maid's key, let himself into the Strauss household when its owner was there alone, dropped an old Sauber clock into the bath, found the key to the bureau, and searched in vain for something he believed it contained.

When the detective subsequently heard that the tinker had moved to the district where the Sauber workshop was situated, he made the reasonably safe assumption that those premises would be the next target. He was correct, and the tinker was apprehended.

The man pleaded guilty to breaking and entering but not to murder. In his defence, he gave what he swore was a true account of what had happened.

His name was Wolfgang Sauber, and back in Switzerland he and his brother Gustav (who was not an orphan – nor was his mother's maiden name Sauber) had designed a highly efficient electric cuckoo clock. The moment the mechanism's teething troubles had been overcome and the clock was ready for commercial development, Gustav disappeared with all their paperwork, including patents and blueprints. Wolfgang had no idea where he had gone nor what he had done until he happened to read in his local library the edition of the *Illustrated London News* featuring the success of his brother's clock-manufacturing business.

Wolfgang immediately saw that Gustav had come to England, changed his name to Strauss, and produced the instrument on his own. As the patent was in the name of Sauber, he was obliged to manufacture it under that name. Now that Wolfgang had discovered how he had been swindled, he began his quest for a share of the Strauss fortune. First, he wrote threatening letters. When these received no reply, he came to Birmingham and made unseasonal cuckoo calls to warn Gustav of his presence and frighten him into agreeing to a settlement. Again meeting with a rebuff, he waited for a suitable opportunity for a confrontation.

Watching the Strauss house carefully, he struck when Lilly and the children were away and the cook had been given two days off. He stole the front door key from the maid's purse, taking a handful of coins to make it look like a conventional robbery. (Feeling sorry for her, he did not take her ten-shilling note.)

Precisely what happened next remains unclear. Wolfgang says he entered the house to find the businessman taking a bath. Wolfgang had with him the prototype cuckoo clock the two of them had designed and built together. The two men argued. While Gustav remained in the bath, the furious Wolfgang wired up the clock and set it going to show that the prototype they had developed together – but which had made a fortune only for Gustav – worked perfectly. Somehow, in the heat of the moment, the clock slipped into the bath, with fatal consequences.

Wolfgang realized the electrocution would be seen as an accident. Seizing the moment, he opened his brother's bureau in the hope of discovering papers showing the clock design was partly his. Finding nothing, he correctly assumed they would be at the Strauss workshop.

Unluckily for him, Sherlock Holmes had come to the same conclusion and was waiting for him.

Watson's notes do not tell us whether Wolfgang Sauber was charged with murder. He does tell us, however, that Lilly Phillips soon got over the loss of her deceitful partner and moved to Salcombe in Devon, where she afterwards lived, happily and legally married, as Mrs Bothwaite.

The Adventure of the Athenian Bust

Holmes and Watson began with the first telegram, the one Bannon sent to Harper. They both got the last date immediately: 1805, the Battle of Trafalgar. Watson then ventured 14:15 as the Battle of Agincourt, and when Holmes added 17:06, the Battle of Ramillies, they began to realize that all the dates were probably battles. And so it turned out.

Some dates, such as 1805, were tricky because there was more than one famous battle in that year, but by trying different alternatives they quickly cracked the code to reveal this:

15:25   Pavia
15:71   Lepanto
14:15   Agincourt

04:80	Thermopylae
17:08	Oudenarde
18:54	Inkerman
18:15	New Orleans
12:63	Largs
18:98	Omdurman
16:45	Naseby
16:50	Dunbar
13:88	Otterburn
18:27	Navarino
12:98	Falkirk
04:26	Olpae
18:79	Ulundi
17:06	Ramillies
18:12	Salamanca
16:42	Edgehill
17:09	Poltava
18:05	Trafalgar

The next step was simple: the initial letter of each entry spelled

PLATOINLONDONFOURSEPT

or

PLATO IN LONDON FOUR SEPT

Using the same process, Holmes decoded Harper's reply:

17:04	Blenheim
16:43	Roundway Down
18:49	Isaszeg

18:76	Little Bighorn
17:75	Lexington
03:33	Issus
17:99	Abukir
17:00	Narva
18:09	Talavera
13:46	Crécy
12:17	Lincoln
04:89	Isonzo
12:65	Evesham
17:98	Nile
17:59	Ticonderoga
16:58	Dunes
18:07	Eylau
18:13	Leipzig
02:06	Ilipa
18:63	Gettysburg
10:66	Hastings
14:61	Towton
18:00	Engen
13:32	Dupplin Moor

This gave them

BRILLIANTCLIENTDELIGHTED

or

BRILLIANT CLIENT DELIGHTED

The plot was now clear.

When a rival collector had approached John Harper and offered to pay handsomely for his assistance in getting hold of the rare bust of Plato, the young man was sorely tempted. He discussed the matter with his sweetheart, Philippa Bannon, and the couple decided to accept the offer. It was the only way they could get enough capital to marry and set up home together. Neither had family money and, as Mrs d'Arche had noted, they could not possibly run a household of any comfort on their meagre salaries.

John Harper made most of the arrangements when he first met with the archaeologist. For a considerable fee from the gazumping collector (on top of the tidy sum the d'Arches would already be paying him) the Albanian agreed to deliver the bust to the yacht, and then secretly remove it again for shipping to England in Mr Harper's name. Told the date of arrival by Bannon, Harper would present himself at the London docks, take possession of the crate, and deliver it to his paymaster. The plan might have worked had not four hefty police officers, alerted by a telegram from Sherlock Holmes, been waiting for him at the quayside.

Philippa Bannon's role was two-fold. First, to tell Harper in a coded telegram when the stolen case was arriving (4 September). Second, to ensure no one was around when the Albanian and his two assistants, the same trio that had delivered the case, came on board to carry it away again at 3 a.m. the following morning.

Generous servings at the drinks reception ensured the

d'Arches slept heavily. Bannon silenced the butler, the maids, the captain, and the crew with gifts ('please don't tell anyone; this is just a little thank-you from me') of their favourite tipples – whisky in the case of the butler and the captain, port for the maids, and rum for the sailors. The next morning's sore heads were not just the result of Mr d'Arche's shouting.

When Holmes knocked on the door of Bannon's cabin and asked to borrow her history books, she had known the game was up. She hastily collected what little money she had and, while the detective and his friend were working on deciphering the telegrams, she slipped ashore and disappeared. The d'Arches made no effort to trace her. With Plato safely on his plinth in the long gallery, they no longer had any interest in Philippa Bannon whatsoever.

The Mystery of the Vanishing Philatelists

When Watson asked Holmes what made him suspect Reverend Woolfstein of responsibility for the murder of the three philatelists, the detective smiled and said the three murdered men, contrary to what their wives and the landlady of the Golden Swan believed, were not philatelists. They were enthusiastic members of the National Secular Society, a group of freethinkers dedicated to bringing down all organized religion. They pretended to be members of a non-existent Newington Stamp Society to avoid upsetting their wives and so as not to fall out with the Anglican landlady of their meeting place. (This is also why their wives never saw the stamp collections.) It was not albums they took to their meetings but piles of freethinking literature, such as the mocking compendium, *Woman, Her Glory, Her Shame, and Her God* by 'Saladin'.

This explains why the three men eagerly challenged Woolfstein when he preached outside the Golden Swan. The leaflets the landlady saw them handing out were those of the National Secular Society, not the Newington Stamp Society. The freethinkers' open challenge to Woolfstein's fanatical beliefs and authority drove him to arrange for their murder. But blasphemers had to perish in a biblical manner.

Holmes remembered that Woolfstein's headquarters was called the Temple of Christ Revealed. He realized the significance of the last word when he heard the preacher chastise the woman who had opposed him. The phrase 'Babylon is fallen', he recalled, came from the Book of Revelation as it appeared in the King James Bible. He had gone on to tell his critic to 'heed the Book of Revelation', too.

On reading the text for himself, Holmes reflected upon the dates of the three men's disappearance: Jack Durrant on 16 June – or June 16 in the USA: 6.16; Gregory Billings on 5 September – or September 5: 9.5; and John Coleman on 5 November – or November 5: 11.5. Their mutilated bodies appeared in the street on 8 November – November 8: 11.8.

Once he had examined the bodies, Holmes confirmed his suspicion by checking that the method of each killing matched the relevant chapter and verse in the Book of Revelation. He was not disappointed:

Revelation 6.16: *And said to the mountains and rocks, Fall on us* … Jack Durrant was crushed to death.

Revelation 9.5: … *and their torment was as the torment of a scorpion, when he striketh a man.* Gregory Billings died of multiple scorpion stings.

Revelation 11.5: … *fire proceedeth out of their mouth, and devoureth their enemies: and if any man will hurt them, he must in this manner be killed.* John Coleman was burned to death.

And finally, Revelation, Chapter 11, Verse 8: *And their dead bodies shall lie in the street of the great city* … The corpses of the three freethinkers were gruesomely arranged in Colombo Street.

The police search of the Temple of Christ Revealed uncovered a secret underground room in which Durrant, Billings and Coleman had been done to death. The iron weights used for the first murder were still there, as were ashes of the fire in which Coleman had perished. The cage used to bring in the scorpions that stung Billings lay empty in a corner. One of the guilty men confessed that when they were unable to tempt the creatures back into their cage after

Billings had died, they crushed them with brooms and threw them into the Thames.

Had they done the same with the bodies of the blasphemers they had slain, he mused, they might still be at liberty. But Woolfstein had forbidden such a move. It would be, he said, contrary to the Holy Bible, the revealed word of God.

A Case of Bananas

On reading of the verdict in the *Daily Chronicle*, Holmes had thrown the newspaper down in disgust and declared the coroner to be a fool. The report made him doubly suspicious, he explained to Watson. One spider hidden within bunches of bananas was rare enough; two in the same hiding place was almost unheard of. To confirm his suspicion of foul play, the detective took down a volume of the *Encyclopaedia Britannica* from the shelves and turned to the article on spiders.

'Just as I thought,' he declared in triumph. 'The only seriously venomous, deadly spider of the Americas is the Brazilian wandering spider of the *Phoneutria* genus. As its common name indicates, the creature is found in South and Central America, not in the Caribbean. There is, my dear Watson, therefore only one explanation for a pair of these vile creatures being found together in a shipment of bananas from Jamaica. Someone must have put them there with criminal intent.'

The 'someone' was eventually discovered to be George Gilbertson, aided and abetted by Dorothy Matteson. The couple had love but no money. Unwilling to live in both sin and penury, they planned to do away with Mr Matteson, from whom Dorothy stood to inherit £150,000, in order to enjoy a life of respectable luxury together. And so they might, had not Sherlock Homes happened upon that report in the *Daily Chronicle*.

Murder in Room 327

The true story of the murder in room 327, as revealed by Sherlock Holmes, was as follows.

Albert Higginbottom, a brutal but wealthy manufacturer of ammunition and small arms, married Agnes Walker in July 1878. She had accepted his marriage proposal, against the earnest wishes of her dear twin brother Tom, as he had promised to help her father with his financial difficulties. He reneged on his promise immediately they were wed.

Agnes and Tom's dislike of Higginbottom, fuelled by his cruel treatment of her, came to a head when, on a visit to her doctor to see if she was pregnant, she was told she was not carrying a child but rather the disease syphilis.

When she confronted her husband with this, he assaulted her, beating her about the body, dislodging two of her teeth and breaking her arm.

Tom, temporarily living in the same house as his sister, was incandescent with rage. He took a Higginbottom bayonet, an unsold sample the manufacturer kept in the house, followed his brother-in-law to London, and observed his movements in and out of the Royal Staffordshire Hotel. Noting that the prostitute Maggie Jones was not so different in stature from himself, he devised the plan of replacing the woman for her Thursday night tryst with Higginbottom – and ridding his beloved sister of her vicious husband.

Had the case been solely in the hands of Detective Grimes, Maggie Jones might well have been hanged. Fortunately for her, Sherlock Holmes was not so easily deceived.

Whose arm had been set? he wondered. Which resident of Sheffield would Higginbottom be most likely to pay for? The answer was surely his wife. The chances of this being the case increased considerably when Dr Gumpert's reply to Holmes's telegram confirmed he had set the arm of a 'lady'.

If this lady was indeed Agnes Higginbottom, how had she broken her arm? Marital discord was certainly a possibility, especially when considering the probable reaction of a newly-wed bride to her husband's syphilis. This unpleasant scenario might account for the scratches on Higginbottom's body, inflicted some time before his death.

Holmes also reasoned that a physical confrontation between Mr and Mrs Higginbottom, resulting in injury to the weaker party, would additionally explain why she was unable to travel to London. Moreover, if she had been hurt but was unwilling to draw attention to her injuries lest they furnish a motive for her wanting to be rid of her abusive husband, she would need an excuse for not travelling. Hence the story, which the police telegram revealed to be false, about the cab accident.

Two facts from the scene of the crime fuelled Holmes's suspicions. Why would Higginbottom have brought an obsolete bayonet with him when he was on a mission to sell ammunition? Perhaps the killer had introduced the murder weapon into the room? That would limit the number of suspects to those who could easily have got hold of discontinued bayonets and placed Mrs Higginbottom and her brother at the top of the list. Then there was the power of the murder blow: surely a thrust of such force could only have been performed by a man?

Continuing his line of thought, Holmes wondered why Agnes's telegram had said Tom was not free to travel to London straight away. One possibility was that he had not yet *returned* from the capital. And who was the youthful-looking figure who had changed from male to female clothing, and back again, in the public conveniences at St

Pancras station? From the description Holmes had been given of a 'girly-looking man', he sounded remarkably like the youth Holmes had seen in the wedding photograph. And if it were him, wouldn't that explain why the 'woman' visiting Higginbottom on the night he was murdered had been unwilling to speak?

Finally, was poor Maggie Jones's explanation of why she did not go to the hotel on Thursday night so implausible? If the 'baby-faced gentleman with a northern accent' was who Holmes thought he was, it made perfect sense for him to have paid Maggie not to visit her client that night.

No single answer to any one of Holmes's questions led him unequivocally to the guilty party. But taken together, when he had answered them all rationally and logically, he could reach only one conclusion. Tom Walker, not Maggie Jones, had murdered Albert Higginbottom.

'Bah!' retorted Grimes when the jury found Walker guilty. 'Just beginner's luck, old boy!'

The Fraudster's Finger

Holmes quickly saw that the random letters were a simple scytale. He wrote out the letters in a single line, cut this to a long strip, experimented with spacing and letter size, and wrapped the strip round the shaft of a bulger (now known as a 'driver') golf club, with the letter T at the top. By making the letters small enough for five vertical columns around the circumference of the shaft, he was able to read the following:

TARGETINDRIVEFIVEFIFTEENPMTHURSDOUG

or

TARGET IN DRIVE FIVE FIFTEEN PM THURS DOUG

Douglas ('Doug') Telford had provided the kidnappers with Vaultson's precise movements. One of them had kept this coded information in his jacket pocket together with the ransom note. In his haste to get away, he had thrown them together into the coach.

Confronted by his clear guilt, Douglas Telford explained that the ransom plot was the work of a group of desperate men ruined by Vaultson's fraudulent money-making scheme. They persuaded Telford, whose father had also been bankrupted by Everyman's Wealth Generator, to take up the post of tutor at Fortune Towers and provide them with information on the millionaire's movements.

The Vaultson family agreed to keep Telford's role in the conspiracy secret if he revealed the names of the gang. This he duly did, and they were passed on to the police. A series of raids swiftly followed, leading to the release of Umbrigg Vaultson and the arrest of his captors.

The day after his dismissal from his post as tutor, Telford received a letter from Sherlock Holmes. Inside was a cheque for £100 accompanied by a note hoping the gift would enable him to stay on the right side of the law in future.

The Mystery of the Missing Masterpieces

Stolen paintings, Holmes knew, would immediately be taken from their frames. Where might the canvasses then be concealed? The simplest place would be behind other paintings of similar size – but that was too obvious. A subtler hiding place was needed. What better than within antique furniture bought in a London saleroom, especially as the count had exported such items several times in the past?

To make the operation doubly secure, the count arranged to be seen buying the furniture in public, at a Gibbins and Dang auction. To this effect, he masterminded an extremely subtle deception.

The thieves, who were apprehended shortly after the plot was uncovered, confessed to having stolen the paintings 'at the request of an unknown foreign gentleman'. They left them, as instructed, in a warehouse in the East End of London. They were removed from their frames shortly afterwards and taken to the workshop of a master carpenter who had come to London from Budapest to seek his fortune. Awestruck by the very name of Count Végh, and terrified by veiled threats about what would happen to his family back home if he refused, he undertook to hollow out parts of the frames of four pieces of furniture brought to him 'for repair' from the count's London home. The stolen paintings were then inserted into the hollows and the furniture reassembled. The vendor's name and address given to Gibbins and Dang turned out to be fictitious.

Once Holmes learned that the count had recently sent furniture for repair, he knew his concealment hypothesis was likely to be correct. In the sale room, he identified four items of furniture with pieces of timber long and thick enough to act as cases for the missing canvasses: the largest one in the *chaise longue*, the smallest in the table, and the other two in the backs of the chairs. Examination with a magnifying glass showed recent careful work on the four suspect items. Lifting the two chairs revealed that they were slightly but significantly lighter than those whose timber was intact.

The acid test was the auction itself. Holmes knew that if the stolen paintings really were concealed in furniture, the count had to buy them, whatever their price. The antics of Vincent de Béarn confirmed this. As the Frenchman correctly observed on leaving the sale room, the Louis XV chairs were indeed worth a great deal more than the count had paid for them.

The Case of the Beaded Egg

Holmes first wrote the notes played by Smith's musical box in conventional form, using a treble clef and a staff of five lines. He then wrote down just the notes:

ACECAFEFACECAGEFADEDEGGDABDEADBEEBEAD

He immediately recognized this as:

ACE CAFÉ

FACE CAGE

FADED EGG

DAB DEAD BEE BEAD

… which is what he did – and the diamond was duly revealed!

The Mystery of the Fallen Sergeant

Holmes knew that the case against Garfield-Wolkes would be difficult to prove in a court of law. He therefore presented the dean, whom he knew to be a man of conscience, with the article for the *New England Telegraph* (a fictitious newspaper) in the hope that it would provoke him to confess. In a way, it did, though not in the manner the detective had intended. He told Watson afterwards that posting the article rather than going to see Garfield-Wolkes in person was one of the few regrets of his long professional career.

On first taking up the case, Holmes set himself the task of answering Blean's three questions.

1. How had Melrose got into the cathedral? If he had not broken in, then he must either have stolen a key or been let in by one of the keyholders. As no key was found on his person, the latter option was the most plausible.

    Once the two canons and the verger had been ruled out, only Garfield-Wolkes remained. The dean and Melrose had army backgrounds and Holmes's research revealed that both had fought in the Third Ashanti War. The chances were, then, that they knew each other.

2. Why was Melrose wearing an empty money belt? The only reason people wore such accoutrements was to carry large sums securely and secretly. Either Melrose had brought money into the cathedral or he was planning to take some out with him. Either way, the dean was involved.

    The chances of a relatively poor man bringing money to pay a wealthy one were remote, Holmes decided. If Melrose was expecting to receive payment from Garfield-Wolkes, what was it for? The only thing the sergeant had to sell was his silence. In other words, he was blackmailing Garfield-Wolkes – he knew something the dean desperately wanted kept secret.

Both *The Times* and the *Telegraph*, Holmes discovered, made reference to allegations of a massacre of Ashanti civilians by one or more members of the Royal Welsh. The subsequent investigation produced no concrete evidence of who was responsible, though strong suspicions remained. Did Melrose know Garfield-Wolkes had participated in the massacre and was taking money from him to keep quiet? If that were so, the sergeant's final message was not one of faith but of accusation: he was trying to write the word 'massacre'. That would explain the strange squiggle after the final S. Melrose had not died attempting a full stop but trying to tell the world the truth about the dean.

3. Melrose's reason for being in the clerestory and not the crypt was now clear: he had gone to an office in the tower to meet with the dean. The thief was not the philandering sergeant but the passionate clergyman: the man had little money of his own, as his wife revealed, and was stealing the plate to meet his blackmailer's escalating demands.

    Holmes deduced that Garfield-Wolkes went to London Bridge rather than Victoria (the obvious terminus for Lambeth Palace) because the former was nearer the city's silver market. In those discreet offices he could get a good price for the stolen items before going on to meet with the archbishop.

At the midnight meeting in the tower, the fiery cleric had finally snapped. Beside himself with rage and guilt, he hurled his blackmailer over the low parapet on to the floor far below. To make it look as if Melrose had fallen while stealing cathedral plate, he then threw down a chalice beside the body.

That, at least, was how the story was to be presented to readers of the *New England Telegraph*. Judging by Dean Garfield-Wolkes's grim response, it was probably pretty close to the truth, too.

The Mystery of the Three Tipsy Clerks

Elijah Petrel's belief that Amir Asaduddin Khan had murdered his two friends was based on supposition and blind prejudice. Holmes saw through this straight away. Khan's speech revealed him to be a highly educated man who, unless he were effecting a sophisticated double bluff, could never have written the misspelled, semi-literate note found by Petrel on his doorstep. Nor would a devout Muslim, as evinced by his references to Allah and the Prophet, have written a message on the label of a beer bottle.

The true author of the threat was identified by his handwriting, backed up by the presence in his room of the stub of a blue pencil and three beer bottles without labels. Confronted with this evidence, Blanket had confessed.

Holmes had begun his investigation by asking himself why an Indian might urgently want to buy a ring from a London pawn shop. The likely premise, he decided, was that the jewel had been stolen in India, and the would-be purchaser was seeking to retrieve it. That, more or less, turned out to be correct.

Holmes learned that two years previously a famous ruby and diamond ring – the Light of Rajasthan – had been taken from the palace of Prince Abdullah Abdelrahman. Servants implicated in the theft confessed to receiving money from an anonymous English soldier. An enquiry was held, and the barracks of the Seventeenth Foot, which was stationed near the palace at the time, were thoroughly searched. The Light of Rajasthan was never recovered, and the Seventeenth Foot returned to England.

Meanwhile, Prince Amir Asaduddin Khan, a Harrow-educated man of the highest caste, had fallen passionately in love with Princess Noor, Prince Abdullah's only daughter. She was equally besotted by him, and the couple asked her father if they might marry. He agreed, on one condition: Khan must recover the Light of Rajasthan and present it to his Princess.

Khan read up about the theft and concluded the ring was in England. Accordingly, he wrote to his English friends and asked them to keep an eye out for it. When an old school friend got in touch to say he'd seen what looked like the missing ring in a London pawn shop, Khan immediately sailed for England.

As we know, he arrived too late to redeem the jewel. From the conversation overheard in the pawn shop, Blanket gathered how desperately Khan wanted the ring, and he determined to sell it to him for a very considerable price. But first he had to get it back from the three clerks …

After Blanket's arrest, Elijah Petrel graciously handed the coveted ring over to Khan. As an expression of his gratitude, Khan gave the clerk £150 in gold and an invitation, all expenses paid, to what turned out to be one of the most glorious weddings India had ever witnessed.

The Adventure of Old Dodson

Dodson had made the simplest of errors, assuming breakfast at six-thirty meant six-thirty a.m. In fact, having spent the night with Miss Hogarth and then murdering her to avoid paying the blackmail money she was demanding, Cannizzaro had returned to his Mayfair apartment to rest. Venturing out in the early evening, he had explained to Delius Graftule, a waiter at the Royal Buckingham who knew him well, that he had only just woken up and required breakfast. Graftule duly obliged and, having received the customary handsome tip, provided his client with the required receipt. Cannizzaro had dictated it word for word, Graftule said, and when he offered to add 'p.m.' after 'six-thirty', he was told it was not necessary.

All this Dodson and Holmes learned within five minutes of their cab arriving at the Royal Buckingham. That left them ample time to proceed to Victoria station, where the detective, assisted by a couple of stout constables, arrested Octavius Cannizzaro, of no fixed abode, on the charge of murdering Miss Fanny Hogarth of Blackheath at 6.30 a.m. that morning. The contents of the victim's jewellery box were found in Cannizzaro's suitcase.

Not content with just taking her life, noted Watson, the heartless villain had also taken back all the precious baubles he had given her.

The Adventure of the
Crooked Draughtsman

The explanation of how Holmes solved the mystery of the draughtsman's code is headed by a rather touching note. 'This is one of the few cases,' Watson wrote, 'in which, albeit inadvertently, I played a significant role in helping my friend bring his deliberations to a satisfactory conclusion.'

As soon as Holmes had the numbers and the initial letters of the positions of the players in a rugby football team before him, the message emerged before his eyes like 'the landscape at sunrise':

LEAVE ARMAMENT TONNAGE SPEED EUSTON

LEFT LUGGAGE SAT SIX THIRTY NAME SCHMIDT

When Herr Schmidt called at Euston station at 6.30 that evening and asked to collect a small briefcase left in his name, the police were waiting for him. Being a man of few moral scruples, he soon divulged the name of his agent in the field: Augustus Gedge. He also revealed that he had asked Gedge to provide him with a secret code for their communications. The draughtsman had come up with the unique rugby code in which the message from his handler had been written. Schmidt confessed that though its bizarre terminology of hookers and props meant nothing to him, he soon got the hang of it and believed Gedge's assurance that it was 'unbreakable' – and so it would probably have remained had it not been for the extraordinary powers of Sherlock Holmes.

Schmidt and Gedge were duly arrested and the law relating to espionage and treason took its stern course. Early the following year, the launching of HMS *Dreadnought*, a revolutionary new battleship, gave Britain an invaluable lead over Germany in the naval arms race that led up to the First World War.

How had Holmes cracked the code?

He had plenty of experience of codes that substituted numbers for letters of the alphabet or vice versa: 1 = A, 2 = B, etc. Set out in full, the arrangement looks like this:

1 = A	10 = J	19 = S
2 = B	11 = K	20 = T
3 = C	12 = L	21 = U
4 = D	13 = M	22 = V
5 = E	14 = N	23 = W
6 = F	15 = O	24 = X
7 = G	16 = P	25 = Y
8 = H	17 = Q	26 = Z
9 = I	18 = R	

The Gedge code involved a double substitution. Instead of A being replaced by 1, it was replaced by the initial letters of the position on the rugby football field that carried the number 1 – in other words the **L**eft **P**rop (LP); so B, being on the jersey of player number 2, was replaced by **H**ooker (H).

Letters beyond O (number 15) were made up of two rugby football positions. For example, W (23) was formed by combining **H**ooker (number 2) and **R**ight **P**rop (number 3), making HR.

Once Holmes had cracked the theory behind the code,

he still had to work out the breaks between the letters and the words. For instance:

For instance: IC / RSR / LP / HH / RSR
        L   E   A   V   E

Set out like this, it looks relatively simple. But, as Holmes admitted to his friend several months later, 'On that occasion, my dear Watson, I have to admit that the solution was, for once, not quite elementary.'

The Adventure of the Eccentric Nephew

When asked about Georgian silver, all but one of the employees realized Holmes was talking about silver from the reign of one of Britain's four kings named George. The odd one out was Gregor de Villiers, who talked about silver from the American state of Georgia. Holmes was immediately reminded that Charlie Peters, the infamous American thief, had been reported sailing to Britain a while back, and he devised a second linguistic trap to confirm his suspicions.

Disguised as the eccentric Horatius Knebb, Holmes had stolen six small objects belonging to Sir Cecil and Lady Mount. He then took each of the servants aside individually and invited them to join his game: that night, when no one was around, would they take the object he was about to give them and hide it in a trunk in the stables? The mission was top secret and they must tell no one, not even their fellow servants. All agreed to do what he wanted.

The five British servants hid their objects in the sea chest – or 'trunk' in British English – at the back of the garage. Peters hid his object, the corsets, in the car's luggage compartment, known in America as a 'trunk'. The action confirmed his American (rather than South African) identity, after which the rest of the case was swiftly wrapped up.

As Holmes remarked to Watson afterwards, 'despite the confusion they cause, the linguistic differences between Britain and the United States do sometimes have their uses'.

The Case of the Frowning Lady

After Mrs Latchcombe had made her way out of Holmes's rooms, still frowning, Watson expressed his dismay at his friend's lack of chivalry towards a lady in distress. The detective assured the doctor that he would be the first to come to the rescue of anyone in genuine distress, but he was not sure anything about the self-styled 'Mrs Latchcombe' was genuine.

Watson asked him to explain.

Crucially, as Watson had himself deduced on first meeting her, the woman frowned because she was severely myopic and was too vain to wear spectacles in public. That explained why she mistook Watson for Holmes when she first came in, and had to feel for a chair before sitting down.

Once her myopia had been ascertained, her story of the robbery fell to pieces. She came out of the bathroom with wet hair over her face – clearly not wearing spectacles, therefore – yet she said she had identified a robber more than ten yards away on the other side of her drawing room. Moments later, she was apparently able to see a clenched fist and pearl necklace at an even greater distance.

These falsehoods called into question the rest of her story. She may well have met and married a Lieutenant Latchcombe on leave from India, but had the relationship really led to the conception of a child or was the 'young Albert' a fiction to persuade the lieutenant to return to her? How strange, on coming to see a detective about her case, not to bring a photograph of her child. Furthermore, what reputable boarding school accommodated pupils in early August?

No, Holmes concluded, there was no way of telling whether anything the sad and lonely lady had said was true. She may well have heard that Latchcombe – back from India or not – was in the vicinity and concocted the theft story in a desperate attempt to blackmail him into returning to her.

Of course she had not gone to the police. The dumbest

constable would have seen through her fabricated tale after the briefest of investigations. Why she thought Sherlock Holmes would swallow it, goodness only knows. He saw through it without needing to leave his chair.

A Case of Ignorance

Many years later, when Watson invited Holmes round for a brandy and a chat about old times, the detective recalled the name of Minnie Dean and the strange conversation he had overheard between her and Ernest Pottinger. He repeated the words verbatim to Watson, asking what he made of them.

'My dear Holmes!' exclaimed his friend. 'How could you have missed it? The wretched woman all but confessed her guilt – and in your hearing, too!'

When Holmes asked what on earth he meant, Watson reached up, took down his copy of Thomas Hardy's *Tess of the d'Urbervilles*, and handed it to his friend. Having outlined the plot,* he asked, 'Perhaps too late to go to the police now, Holmes?'

* Tess, the central character in Thomas Hardy's great late-Victorian novel, is hanged for murdering the man who had taken advantage of her all her life. She is arrested at Stonehenge, hence Ernest's use of 'Stonehenge moment'. Tess's lover is Angel Clare, which is why Minnie had called her lover 'my angel'. Saying she was 'hardier' than Tess was an obvious pun on the name of the author, Thomas Hardy ('Old Tom').

The detective nodded. 'Besides, Watson,' he added, 'though she may have pushed that bounder into a quarry, I think he had done more than his fair share of pushing around, don't you?'

The Case of the Surgeon's Secret

In explaining his reasoning, Holmes mildly rebuked Lord Frogmore on two counts. First, for not getting to know the Axelsons better before asking Agnes to marry him. Second, for being so old-fashioned in his assumptions.

In the twentieth century, Holmes pointed out, the occupation of surgeon was not limited to men, especially in the United States. The mention of the name 'Axelson' had reminded him of an article he had read on the subject. In it he had learned that Mrs Henrietta Axelson was one of a small but significant number of pioneer women surgeons who graduated from the New York Medical College for Women in the latter part of the nineteenth century – in other words, Agnes Axelson had been operated on by her own mother.

So of course the young woman would always love her surgeon with all her heart, Holmes smiled, even when married to her equally dear Edward.

The Adventure of the Archway Operator

The police made the mistake of seeing the entries in the notebook – as Yendle had intended – as simple telephone numbers. In other words, they attempted to link PADDINGTON with 707, etc.

Holmes avoided the obvious and focused instead on the heading, 'Agreement'. Once he had done this, he saw he was looking at a sort of criminal contract setting out how the gang were to divide up their ill-gotten gains. The percentages beneath each column, he realized, meant they should be treated separately. If a name was concealed in the list of telephone exchanges, and another name in the list of numbers, then the figures beneath (30 per cent and 15 per cent) must represent how the loot from the raids was to be split. By implication, the largest share (55 per cent) was allocated to the gang leader, Yendle.

The column of exchanges was easily deciphered. The initial letters spelled the name HAMPDEN. Jimmy Hampden, an old colleague of Yendle's whom the police mistakenly believed had fled to Australia, was found hiding in a cellar in Hackney. Never having received much of an education, Hampden probably thought Yendle's simple puzzle would be sufficient to disguise his identity.

The name concealed in the numbers was more obscure. Holmes noticed that the sums of the final digits were: 23, 19, 20, 5, 20, 18 and 1. As in 'The Case of the Crooked Draughtsman', the detective swiftly identified these numbers as corresponding to letters of the alphabet on the basis A = 1, B = 2, etc. This gave him an easy anagram to solve – STEWART – 23 = W, 19 = S, 20 = T, 5 = E, 20 = T, 18 = R, 1 = A. Once the name had emerged, the police were able to take over.

Charles Murray Stewart was an Old Etonian who had provided the gang with firearms smuggled into the country from Ireland. As a man of education, he had insisted that the makeshift contract disguise his name in a subtler way than a straightforward anagram. Subtle it might have been, but not sufficiently so to fox Sherlock Holmes. Stewart was drowned when his yacht, pursued by a police launch, ran into rocks close to the Needles lighthouse and was smashed to pieces.

ACKNOWLEDGEMENTS

I am hugely grateful to Ellie Ross, Lucy Ross, Louise Dixon and my editor, George Maudsley, for their help and advice with the manuscript.